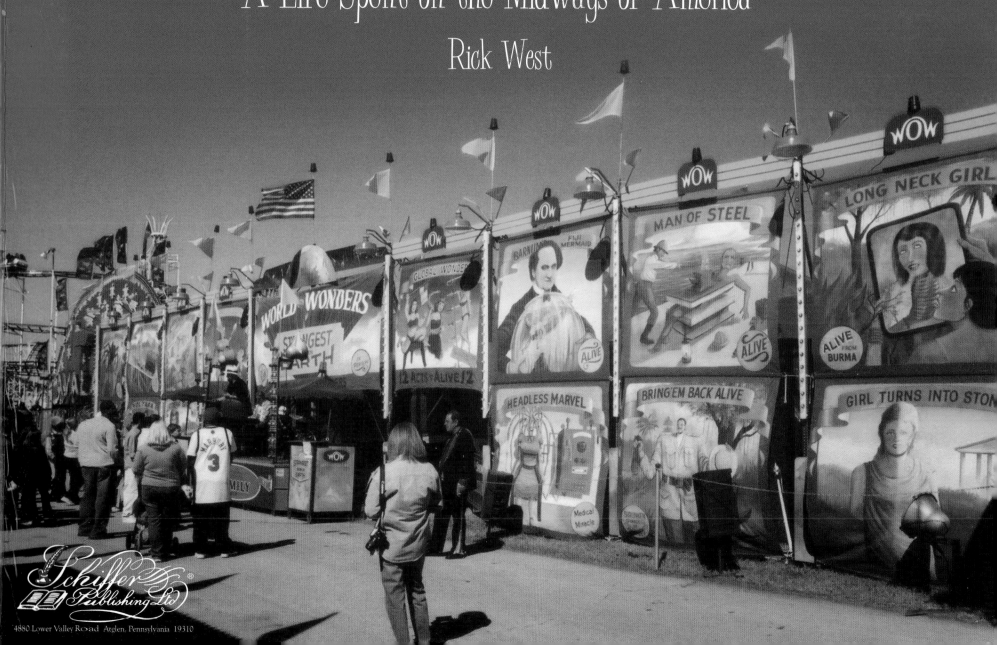

PICKLED PUNKS AND GIRLIE S

A Life Spent on the Midways of America

Rick West

Schiffer Publishing Ltd

4880 Lower Valley Road Atglen, Pennsylvania 19310

Other Schiffer Books on Related Subjects:

Midget Exhibit: Images from the Heyday of Dwarf Display,
978-0-7643-2114-5

Copyright © 2011 by Rick West

Library of Congress Control Number: 2011920563

Designed by Bruce Waters
Type set in Academy/Caxton Bk BT

ISBN: 978-0-7643-3703-1
Printed in China

Schiffer Books are available at special discounts for bulk purchases for sales promotions or premiums. Special editions, including personalized covers, corporate imprints, and excerpts can be created in large quantities for special needs. For more information contact the publisher:

Published by Schiffer Publishing Ltd.
4880 Lower Valley Road
Atglen, PA 19310
Phone: (610) 593-1777; Fax: (610) 593-2002
E-mail: Info@schifferbooks.com

For the largest selection of fine reference books on this and related subjects, please visit our website at **www.schifferbooks.com**
We are always looking for people to write books on new and related subjects. If you have an idea for a book please contact us at the above address.

This book may be purchased from the publisher.
Include $5.00 for shipping.
Please try your bookstore first.
You may write for a free catalog.

In Europe, Schiffer books are distributed by
Bushwood Books
6 Marksbury Ave.
Kew Gardens
Surrey TW9 4JF England
Phone: 44 (0) 20 8392 8585; Fax: 44 (0) 20 8392 9876
E-mail: info@bushwoodbooks.co.uk
Website: www.bushwoodbooks.co.uk

Some of the events in this book are told just as they happened, some are told only as I remember them, and some are told as I wished they had happened. It makes no difference which is which...it's all true.

Rick West

To my wife, Abby, who puts up with all my nonsense.

CONTENTS

FOREWORD

His Life Is the Midway

Before I'd even met him, I knew Rick West. Before I knew his name. Before I'd even heard of him. I knew the kid who'd wanted to be out there, to be *with it and for it*, from almost before he knew what the expression would demand of him. I knew the show folk who lived to give the public what made them glad to come to the carnival, the fair. I knew the showmen who spent every waking moment—the wink wink nudge nudge of the inveterate humbug artist uppermost in their minds—working everything and everyone to ensure their show played as strong as possible. And I knew a fellow historian of the business, knew one at a hundred paces, one who never quite felt comfortable just doing it himself unless he filled his "idle" hours listening to others "cut up the jackies" till long into the night. Didn't know him, hadn't met him, didn't know his name. But I knew Rick West. All I needed was for the man to step into the silhouette.

That man, that Rick West, came to me by way of my *Shocked and Amazed!*, a fairly common way to travel if one is looking to talk sideshow and the backend shows in general. Maybe it was finding a fellow yakker who loved the business, one who had a long history in the business to boot, that made the relationship so fruitful. For whatever reason, it wasn't hard to recognize a kindred spirit and even know his story before this memoir crossed my desk. And what a memoir it is. Much of the "old" midway is gone—those "golden age" sideshows from both circuses and carnivals, remembered so fondly by many, the crime and dope shows, the all-girl reviews, the pickled punk and life shows, the midget reviews and fat shows, the diving horses and high divers, the kooch shows, the monkey speedways, the motordromes, the AT shows. Much of it was gone by the days of Rick West's youth. Fortunately for us, though, not all. Not all, indeed.

When you spend your youth, as Rick West did, lusting after a thing, well, something's gotta give. That "give," as for so many showmen who join on with the show, came early from someone near and dear. For West, it was care of his uncle, one of the last of the freak animal showmen still working the midways. And thanks be to Uncle Tom Beimborn for that. Between them, West and Beimborn exhibited more giant livestock than Ol' McDonald had to farm. And in between, his love for the business pushing him always, West saw and/or sought out more shows and showmen than you, dear reader, have a right to demand of a writer. And thanks be to Rick West for that.

James Taylor
Author, curator, and sideshow historian

Acknowledgments

A great number of people helped and influenced me along the way, and I want to thank you all. I especially want to thank my uncle, Tom Beimborn, known in the business for exhibiting some of the largest, most unforgettable giant steers ever shown, who gave me a start and education in the business; Joe and Karen Cisneroz encouraged me with this project from the very beginning; James Taylor shared valuable publishing information and took time out of his busy schedule to supply the foreword; Al Stencell supplied hard-to-come-by photographs; Mason Loika for his help with editing; Frank Hansen for setting time aside for our interview and allowing me to photograph his infamous Iceman.

Thanks to the Carnival Museum, maintained by the International Independent Showmen's Association in Gibsonton, Florida, for their help; Sylvia Cassidy graciously allowed me to use her photos; Paula Ben Jacobson offered advice and support; Norris Welch, the Monkeyman, allowed me to use some of his colorful jackpots; Alan Hogan permitted me to vicariously participate in his adventures and sent rocks and curios from the far and inaccessible reaches of the world; my cousin Wayne Pies, a fellow showman, helped many times with ideas and bookings; and Ward Hall, "King of the Sideshows," shared incredible stories with Abby and me.

Also, thanks to my mom, Dottie West, for her unwavering support; and to my precious wife, Abby, for her love and encouragement throughout the entire project; and finally, to all the people who helped get my shows on the road over the years: my wife, Abby; Wayne Bradley; Gatorman; Nate Kern; cousins Allen and Bart Vanden Plas; my mom, Dottie West; my sister, Vicki Fieck; Joe & Karen, Joey, Jesse Cisneroz, and Anna (Cisneroz) Beck; Paula "Ben" Jacobson; Dean Vanden Heuval; Teri; Clarence Heidgen; Tom Smith; Alan Hogan; Ricky Lindsley; my cousin Wayne Pies; Dan Glaser; Greg Daily; Tom Smith; Chris and Joanne Englert; Mike Neely; Art Holland; Mike McGarity; Sam Staffen; Bobby Hawk; my dad, R.M. West and his brother, Jack; Bobby Hawk; Mark Palmer; Conley Wilson; Dale Kuipers; Jimmy Daniels; and the many others who helped along the way.

The last fifty years have been a strange and wonderful trip. A big thank you to all who had a hand in making it happen.

CHAPTER I
The First Fair
Seeing Is Believing!

The first fair I ever attended was the Ozark Empire Fair in my hometown of Springfield, Missouri, the "Show Me State." I was five years old at the time, and it is still fresh in my mind, at least parts of it, after more than fifty years.

I was born in Springfield in 1948 and lived with my grandmother Ovel. As she always told everyone, she spelled her name with an "e," not an "a." She was a little lady, only four foot ten inches tall.

My parents lived in a travel trailer in Grandma's back yard on West Walnut Street. But I remember living with Grandma during this time more than with my own parents. Grandma always kept a large number of potted red geraniums on the front porch and raised African violets on a covered back porch. She owned a large piano that she kept in the dining room—it was perfect for me to play under, around, and behind. And she cared for a noisy blue and yellow pet parakeet that she allowed to fly freely around the house. If Grandma wanted the parakeet to be quiet, she would put the bird in its cage and cover the cage with a towel. I loved watching that parakeet take a bath in the kitchen sink!

Future showman Rick West decked out in his Gene Autry cowboy outfit, 1952.

Rick on Grandma Ovel's back porch steps, 1952.

8

Her parents, my great grandparents Edward and Lizzie Anderson, were farmers in the Ozark Mountains. Grandma had taken me out to their rocky-hill farm many times. The farm was located in southwestern Missouri, a half mile from Stinson in Lawrence County. There was no television as most homes have now, but they did have a big tabletop radio and a wood-cased telephone that hung on the kitchen wall. If you turned the crank on the side, another phone would ring at someone else's house. Their party line only went to one other place, my Aunt Oral's farm, half a mile down the road. That's because my grandfather, Edgar, a lineman for the phone company, put up a private line between the two farms. The connection wasn't all that great. It sounded like you were using two cans connected with a string.

Great grandparents Edward and Lizzie Anderson with daughters Ovel and Oral, Stinson, Lawrence County, Missouri, 1912.

Great grandparents Edward and Lizzie Anderson, 1955.

My great grandparents got all their water from a 15-foot-deep, hand-dug well. I can remember going out to draw water from it. There was a rope with a bucket on it, just like in the cowboy movies. A bucket of water was kept on the screened-in back porch with a blue-and-white enameled dipper in it. That was some of the best water I ever tasted. My great granddad always wore bib overalls. He was the only tall person in the family, and had a great head of silver hair.

The floors in the house, all covered in linoleum with throw rugs, had settled and sagged in every room. The farmhouse had a particular smell that I have since associated with old people and old houses. All kinds of flowers were planted around the house, attracting a large number of hummingbirds and butterflies. I don't know how my great grandmother, Lizzie, found time to do all the flower planting, with the farm work and all. The road out in front was gravel and got so hot in the summer I could hardly stand to walk on it barefoot. Nevertheless, I was constantly out exploring the fields and woods when we went to the farm. After the fertile bottomland along the creek was plowed, the next rain would uncover arrowheads in the freshly turned soil. I accumulated quite a collection of arrowheads as a kid.

My grandma had a large, purple birthmark on her face. Her mom told her a neighbor's house had burned when she was carrying Ovel, and the act of putting her hand to her face in astonishment caused the birthmark to appear on her unborn child. I'm not sure if Grandma believed that or not, but a lot of people did believe in that sort of thing.

Rick's grandma Ovel at Lake Nacogdoches, 1981.

smell of musty, mildewed tent canvas; livestock displays featuring horses, hogs, and cattle; freshly baled hay; tractors; caramel apples; pitchmen; and the sideshows.

Of all the sights and sounds I remember, the sideshows called to me the loudest. The shows were so big and beautiful, with lots of red and yellow lettering on the banners. And the talker on the platform out front had the most amazing stories to explain what you were going to see on the inside... "something you have never seen before." And the pictures and signage on banners in the front of the shows were, just as they said, "unbelievable, incredible, amazing, educational, exotic, a once in a lifetime opportunity." Someone was even showing a two-headed baby! (Out in front of the show a baby buggy was parked next to the stage, and just above the buggy there was a sign that read, "Born to live.") The talker (carnies never call him a barker) was out front working the crowd:

Ladies and gentlemen, on the inside you will see the most unusual child in the world. A child born, not with one head like you and me, but a child born with two heads. Created by God, not by the hand of man. Doctors and nurses will be permitted to enter free with proper credentials. Cashiers, put away the adult tickets...for the next two minutes, and only two minutes, everyone goes on a child's ticket of twenty-five cents. If you are in line, you are in time...enter on the price of a child's ticket. Now's the time to go! Don't wait, don't hesitate, go now!

I wanted to get in line, but Grandma was not going to pay twenty-five cents to let her five-year-old grandson see a freak two-headed baby. I pointed out it was educational—a once in a lifetime opportunity—just as I heard the man on the stage describe it. And more importantly, I really wanted to see it! "Come on, Grandma, please," I pleaded. Grandma was having no part of it. It wasn't happening, period. Grandma grabbed my hand and started pulling me down the midway. "Darn it," I muttered. I really wanted to see it.

As luck would have it, though, Dollie the two-headed cow was waiting patiently a short distance down the midway, just past the tiny horses that were reportedly captured by Indians in the Grand Canyon. What a stroke of luck! The recorded message blared from the speakers, *"It has a mouth to eat with, and a mouth to drink with. Look into her four big brown eyes."* This wasn't as good as a two-headed baby, but a two-headed anything was pretty neat!

Maternal impressions, or psychic imprinting, is the belief that what a pregnant woman sees, eats, or experiences can cause corresponding alterations in her unborn fetus. The belief was universally accepted well into the 1900s and used to explain birth defects, such as the Elephant Man (Joseph Merrick). An elephant supposedly frightened Merrick's mother when she was carrying him, causing his deformity.

But I was telling you about my first fair. It was filled with wonderful sights, sounds, and smells—the calliope music playing at the merry-go-round; hotdogs and hamburgers cooking; cotton candy (the sweet smell was so strong you could almost taste it by the smell alone—just walking by caused your blood sugar to rise!); popcorn; rides; games that agents enticed you to play; flower displays; saltwater taffy being pulled; the

After a little pleading, Grandma gave in this time and bought a ticket, but just one. She didn't want to see a two-headed cow. I handed the man my ticket and ran into the show. There it was... a real, live two-headed cow! It was amazing. Of course, I wanted one. It wasn't as perfect as the one painted on the banner out front. And it was a little hard to see all four big brown eyes, but I could see two faces. (I found out later in life, the shows were never quite as good as the banners depicting them, but that's show business for you.)

I must have been in the show half an hour. People came and went as I questioned the caretaker, "Where did you get it? What do you feed it? How old is it? Where are you going next? How many people come in a day? How much do you make?

"I was wondering if I could get a job with you. I could take care of the cow and answer questions."

They weren't hiring any five-year-old kids. The caretaker finally ran me out of the exhibit as Grandma was hollering, "Ricky, you come on, Ricky."

Darn, it was Grandma's turn. She wanted to see the canned foods and handmade quilts. Grandma grabbed my hand again as we quickly passed by the stage (bally-platform) in front of the girl revue. She didn't even look once at the beautiful, scantily clad, leggy showgirls posing on the stage, or even slow down so I could see what it was all about. Gee, Grandma didn't seem to like the carnival midway too much.

As Grandma tugged me toward the canned foods and quilts, we stopped by the root beer tent. Hundreds of honeybees swarmed all over it, attracted by the root beer's sweet smell. I wanted some too, so Grandma paid a dime for a quart-sized cup. The bothersome bees even tried to get my root beer, but I held my hand over the cup so they couldn't get any.

After seeing the canned foods and quilts, I tried to get Grandma to go past the two-headed baby show again, but it was time to go home. As we headed to the bus stop, I looked back longingly over my shoulder at the colorful midway. Little did I know how much this fair would affect my life!

Rick's grandma Ovel with her dogs, Lawrence County, Missouri, 1907.

11

CHAPTER II
Bozo, the Giant Steer
Grind Shows and Showgirls!

When I was five, my family moved to Ashwaubenon, Wisconsin, a suburb of Green Bay, where I began collecting animals. Some were stored in my bedroom, others in the garage or in cages behind the house. Some of my dogs included a white Spitz and a cocker spaniel, plus I had garter snakes, tortoises, hamsters, birds, rabbits, tropical fish, mice, turtles, and ducks. I would haul almost anything home, including chickens. I would have had a whole zoo, but my folks were always trying to limit the amount of livestock I hauled home.

One summer, I bought four white king pigeons. White Kings are almost as big as chickens, and all white, as the name implies, with red eyes. These giant birds messed up the black shingles of our house; white droppings literally covered the roof.

To get rid of the mess my dad, Bob, hauled the pigeons out to the country and released them. The pigeons flew back home before Dad could get back! The next day Dad said he was going to haul the birds farther away so they couldn't find their way home. This time, they didn't come back. Well, those birds could find their way home from just about anywhere, so I suspect there's more to this story, including fowl play!

Rick with two snapping turtles he caught at Pamperin Park, Brown County, Wisconsin, 1962.

Rick's cages and white king pigeons behind his folk's house on Oneida Street, Green Bay, Wisconsin.

Rick and Bozo at the Outagamie County Fair in Seymour, Wisconsin.

When I was twelve, Tom Beimborn, who was dating my Aunt Frances, became a most influential figure in my boyish life. Tom is charismatic—six feet tall, muscular, and husky, with a commanding voice—he worked for the U.S. Department of Agriculture as a meat inspector covering the state of Wisconsin.

Polaroid photograph of Rick and Bozo, 1960.

My mom, who is deathly afraid of snakes, believes there are only two kinds: rattlesnakes and cobras. When one of my garter snakes escaped and wrapped itself around the front bumper of my family's 1956 Cadillac, Mom called the police. Sure enough, the police showed up at school to escort me home to round up my snake.

Another time while walking to school, I found some field mice playing in the snow. I placed them in a mason jar along with some snow. Well, you might laugh, but I thought they liked snow.

Anyway, I took the mice to school and put the jar inside my desk. I didn't realize the snow would melt, and the mice would drown. Bummer.

The local newspaper had run a story raving about a giant 3,100-pound, red-and-white Holstein steer that had been trucked into Green Bay from out West to be butchered. Tom came up with a brainstorm.

He decided to show the giant steer at county fairs, charge admission to let folks see it and make a fortune. Where he got that idea, I never knew. No one in his family was ever in the carnival business, but Tom bought the giant Holstein. Then he purchased an old Army mess tent to display the steer.

I helped him build a pen out of 2" x 6" and 4" x 4" lumber. The heavy pen was difficult and time consuming to set up, requiring several dozen bolts. This turned out to be a great learning experience, as I realized limiting the number of pieces reduced the time needed to set up a mobile display. Later, when framing my own shows, I was able to reduce the total number of pen parts to only four.

Tom was still hand-lettering the steer's name, Bozo, onto the front of the tent when our first fair, the Outagamie County Fair, opened in Seymour, Wisconsin. Tom hauled all the equipment to the fair, hired a livestock truck to transport the steer and then—to keep his job at the USDA—let my 12-year-old cousin Wayne and me run the show. Hey, we even got paid for this! And he bought each of us a black short-sleeve shirt, black jeans, a cowboy belt and cowboy hat.

It rained hard the second night of the fair. The top of our tent leaked, and after the show closed we found ourselves traipsing through six inches of standing water. Wayne and I were tired, and we decided to sleep on some straw bales inside the dairy barn; at least the roof didn't leak.

The bales of straw were lined up directly behind the cows, but we never considered the ramifications. You see, dairy cows are known for having loose bowel movements the moment they stand up in their stalls. So in the morning, we awoke to the sounds of every single cow pooping. Cow manure splattered up from the barn floor, covering the straw, Wayne, and myself. I spent the rest of the morning trying to comb the dried cow crap out of my hair.

At the end of the week, Tom arrived with a small, open-topped rental trailer. We tore down the tent and pen, and pulled all the tent stakes, piling everything into the trailer. Tom then hauled the whole kit and caboodle to another fair. Every night after we closed, Wayne and I took Bozo for a walk. The steer had his own ideas though. Can you picture a one-and-a-half-ton steer dragging two scrawny 12-year-old boys through the fair parking lot?

"Hey, you boys need some help?" people hollered.

"No, we got him," we yelled as we flew by.

See Bozo, the world's largest steer. He stands six feet tall and can raise his head to a height well over seven feet. 10,000 hamburgers on the hoof! And he's real. He's alive. You know he's alive, you can smell him. Look through the front door. That's his back you see over the tarp, and he's standing right on the ground. It's only ten cents, one dime. You will never see so-o-o much for so-o-o little!

Sideshows reached their height before the 1960s; even so, most carnivals still had them. Hundreds of sideshows clamored for attention: animal shows, freak shows, what-is-it shows, ten-in-one shows, illusion shows, wax shows, crime shows, snake shows, baby shows, and, of course, girl shows.

"Bozo the World's Largest Steer," walk-through banner created for the 1960 Wisconsin State Fair.

The rides kept getting bigger, brighter, and faster. The double Sky Wheel on Royal American Shows was the first spectacle I remember. Hundred-thousand-dollar rides hadn't taken over the fairs yet, but high-capacity, European-type rides like the Himalaya and Music Fest were coming. A real seer looking into the future could hear the rock music and live DJ yelling, "Do you want to go faster? I can't hear you!"

Royal American Shows' lighted marquee, four-abreast Ferris wheels, and light towers at the 1933 Minnesota State Fair. For over seventy years, all others measured themselves against R.A.S., America's biggest carnival. Started by Carl Sedlmaya in the 1920s, R.A.S. traveled by rail car. In 1977 it became involved in a tax evasion scandal that cost the carnival its Canadian route. R.A.S. then lost some of its most profitable fairs to bidding wars among the major carnivals. Rick's giant horse, Big Jim, was booked on R.A.S. at the Minnesota State Fair in 1984. Competition for the top fairs continues today. In 2002, after playing the North Carolina State Fair in Raleigh for 53 straight years, James E. Strates Shows lost the midway contract to Amusements of America.

It was a fantastic summer, at least as I remember it, and we ended up at the Wisconsin State Fair. "Miss Blaze Fury, the Human Heat Wave" was a huge draw as the featured attraction at Royal American Shows' girl-show revue, Club Lido. The show presented a dozen girls, a band, a comic, and the most beautiful costumes you ever saw.

Royal American Shows' Club Lido with twin sky wheels in the background.

European-styled Himalaya on the James E. Strates Shows.

Out on the bally platform—a flatbed semi-trailer with a ticket box and set of steps on each end—the talker was making his opening. He brought out a few of the scantily clad, high-heeled showgirls to help gather the tip as he started his spiel. Their show tent, with seating for a couple hundred people, was set up directly behind the bally platform. When the talker felt the crowd was ready (that is, ready to buy a ticket), he turned the tip.

This is a show that will make the old feel young and the young feel foolish. Ladies and gentlemen, there is a ticket-taker over here, and a ticket-taker over there... if you're ready to go, we're ready to show. Take it on back, girls. It's showtime!

And the girls strutted off the stage.

When Miss Fury took the stage, flaming tassels were attached to her full breasts. She swung them both in the same direction, or each one in a different direction. And Miss Fury wasn't wearing much more than those flaming tassels either. Needless to say, this 12-year-old boy was pretty impressed not only with Miss Fury, but just getting into the girl show was big stuff!

Cousin Wayne and I had an unbelievably good time at the state fair and came up with new ideas to entertain ourselves every day. We filled a large brass, high-pressure fly-sprayer with water so we could wet down fairgoers who looked over the sidewall of the tent. Hey, they were trying to get a free look at Bozo, the Giant Steer!

As the mooches sneaked a peek over the sidewall, we sprayed them in the face. This was a lot of fun. You bet. Eventually though, we got bored,

Miss Fury's unforgettable flaming tassel act that Rick witnessed as a twelve-year-old at the Wisconsin State Fair in 1960. "Often Imitated Never Equaled," Lucia Parks, aka Miss Blaze Fury, died in 1997.

THE HUMAN HEATWAVE BLAZE FURY OFTEN IMITATED NEVER EQUALLED

He led us out back. "Listen to me, boys," he said. "I don't want anyone going to the fair office with a beef about my exhibit. The office does not want to hear or deal with trouble from anyone's exhibit.

"They want people to have fun at the fair."

"Wayne and I were having fun," I joked, trying to ease the tension.

"Hey!" he said sternly. "No more water, period!"

I thought, "Gosh, you can't even throw a little water on a gawker who's stealing a look at your show."

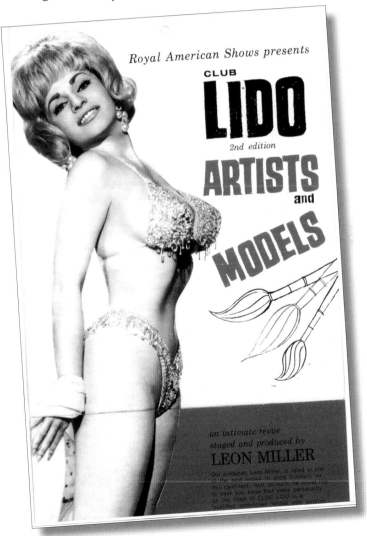

Royal American Shows presents
CLUB
LIDO
2nd edition
ARTISTS
and
MODELS

an intimate revue
staged and produced by
LEON MILLER

1967 program from Royal American Shows' Club Lido, featuring Silvia Cassidy, "Delilah."

so we thought up something else. We stacked a few hay bales by the back corner of the tent (next to where the freeloaders were trying to look in), and stood atop the pile of hay with a full bucket of water. The handle on the bucket dug into my hand, reminding me how wet our next victim was going to find himself.

We waited, but didn't have to wait long. Someone's hands reached up and grabbed the top of the sidewall. I moved one hand to the bottom of the bucket, making sure I steadied the water. I saw a head peek in, it was a man. That's good, we didn't want to drown a lady. The cheapskate began to pull himself up for his free look.

Well surprise, here's a little more than you bargained for, buddy. Two gallons of cold water completely drenched him, and he didn't even get a free look! Man, did we score on this one!

Soaked to the skin, his hair dripping, our victim sulked around to the front of the tent to complain to the owner, my Uncle Tom. Darn, Wayne and I knew we were in trouble now! We listened to Tom apologize to the man for our rude behavior. And watched as Tom give him a dry shirt to wear.

We kept out of sight until the whiner departed, wearing Tom's nice new shirt. We waited for Tom with hearts thumping.

A couple days later, Wayne and I were taking turns sitting at the ticket box.

My turn had come to man the ticket box. Wayne went into Bozo's pen to clean it out, while Tom spoke with a fairly good-sized young man. This guy posed many questions to Tom about the giant steer and how many people we had run through the show. Fifteen or 20 minutes went by, Tom finished talking to the guy, and walked back to help Wayne.

Silvia Cassidy, "Delilah," was a headliner in revues on Royal American Shows, James E. Strates Shows, and Century 21 Shows. She started as a bally girl with Olson Shows.

Silvia Cassidy, the "Girl from the Pearl," headlined for two years in Royal American Shows' Club Lido in the mid-1960s. The revue was produced and choreographed by Leon Miller.

Well, this very same guy was now standing near my left-hand side. I noticed a shadow there, but I didn't pay too much attention to it, because I was busy making change for paying customers. All of a sudden, the creep reached over my shoulder, grabbed the money from the top tray of the cashbox and took off down the midway.

"Help, help, Tom, I've been robbed!" I hollered.

Tom and Wayne came running. Immediately, Tom took over at the ticket box, and Wayne and I took off after the robber. We chased him for a block through the crowded midway but lost sight of him once he ran into the coliseum.

We ran back to tell Tom the bad news.

"You were lucky you didn't catch him," he said. "You would probably have been beat up besides being robbed!"

He was right, of course.

I'm a little embarrassed to even tell you what happened next at the state fair.

Tom sent Wayne and me to the dairy barn to buy some hay. We knew money was tight, and we always tried to help Tom keep the expenses down. Anyway, we took the wheelbarrow and headed for the dairy barn. Wayne and I found a good-sized pile of hay and began loading bales onto the wheelbarrow.

If anyone would say anything to us regarding the hay, we could ask, "Isn't this Tom's hay pile?" Of course, we knew it wasn't, but we could pretend we made an honest mistake and put their hay back. Then we just headed to another pile to "borrow" some hay for Tom. We loaded up the wheelbarrow several times.

After a couple days, Tom found out what we were doing. You guessed it, he did not appreciate our money-saving idea. He told us no more stolen hay, and we had to take back the remaining hay and pay the farmers for what we had used.

Tom asked, "Can't you two stay out of trouble for even one day? No more stolen hay!"

Okay, okay, we made a mistake. Yes, I agree, we were 12 years old and should have known better. We did learn our lesson and never stole any more hay.

When my cousin Wayne and I were not discovering new ways to get ourselves into trouble at the giant steer show, you could find us watching the sideshow and girl-show ballys on the carnival midway or watching the pitchmen hawk their wares in the commercial displays building.

One of the pitches we loved to watch was for the Slice-a-matic. In one part of his spiel, the pitchman would show the crowd how incredibly thin his machine could slice a tomato... so thin you can almost see through it. *"One stingy old woman, bless her heart, sliced a tomato so-o-o thin, it lasted her family the entire winter,"* he told the beguiled onlookers.

Wayne and I would listen to the pitches over and over. After we closed at night we would practice the spiels until we knew them word for word. We even learned the salesman's mannerisms and jokes, nearly mastering the complete routines of a couple pitchmen.

We also enjoyed watching the Jam Auction. A stage was set up to display merchandise on the back end of a straight truck. The rear doors were opened to serve as a backdrop and a gold-colored curtain was hung across the opening to where the merchandise was stored.

A pitchman gathered a tip by tossing free plastic combs, cigarette lighters, pencils, and other cheap trinkets into the crowd of excited fairgoers. *"Here, have one, have one, they're free, given to me to give to you for advertising."* The fairgoers were grabbing and scrambling to get the freebies. As the crowd grew, patrons were directed to move in a little closer to the stage as he would not be able to throw the larger, more expensive items (sewing machines, clocks, lamps, radios, etc.) safely into the audience. After gathering a sizable tip, the pitchman started his spiel, explaining that the company he worked for—*"who by the way paid him handsomely"*—wanted to place this new merchandise into the hands of *"responsible adults for advertising."* He only asked that the recipients tell their friends and neighbors about the wonderful products. (It sounds like the stuff is free, doesn't it?)

I'm not going to go into his whole pitch here but I'll simply state that the lure of "something for nothing" is a strong enticement and has cost many a fair patron a good-sized chunk, if not all, of their paycheck.

Wayne and I watched and studied many other sales pitches, including the car coil, the magic mouse, knifes that never dulled, and cleaning products that could harmlessly remove permanent stains from almost anything. Watching these pitchmen taught us a good deal about the psychology of motivating a mark into spending his hard-earned cash. Good pitchmen even had their customers thanking them after paying for their "too-good-to-be-true" merchandise and trinkets.

When we returned home in the fall, we performed our newly learned routines to the delight of our family and friends. The pitches and spiels from the early 1960s not only fascinated and entertained, they also educated Cousin Wayne and me.

Girlie shows and big show revues were still popular attractions at county fairs during the late 1960s. While I was playing a small fair in Tennessee, I found time to check out the shows that were booked with the carnival. On the back end, where these shows were always located (they even referred to shows as the "back-end"), the "French Casino," a slightly run-down girl show, was in full operation. The show displayed a small, hand-lettered piece of unpainted plywood advertising employment opportunities in show business: "Girls wanted, no experience needed, must be free to travel."

As a couple of the showgirls sashayed out onto the platform and the talker tried to build a tip, I snapped some photographs of the girls and the sign.

French Casino showgirls working the bally next to a crude hand-lettered "Girls Wanted" sign.

Silvia Cassidy and a fellow showgirl relaxing backstage.

The last big girl revue I saw at the county fairs appeared at the Ionia, Michigan, Free Fair in 1974. The show featured "Miss Sandy O'Hara, the Improper Bostonian" in a revue called "Best of Burlesque." *"Everything goes when the whistle blows... it's showtime!"* I had witnessed the end of a long carnival tradition.

Tom married my Aunt Frances, and I worked my way through college by showing one of my new uncle's giant steers each summer. By then, Uncle Tom had three giant steer shows at three different fairs at the same time. As I said, sideshows were big in the 1960s. We played state and county fairs all over the United States and Canada.

One time when we were playing the Ohio State Fair in Columbus, three giant steers owned by three different showmen were on display at the fair. The governor opened the fair by telling reporters, "Our state fair is so big, that we have three World's Largest Steers on display!"

That statement gave the fair a lot of newspaper coverage!

I learned a lot about the business and life in general from my Uncle Tom, at least most of the honest stuff.

An old "Bozo" postcard pitched by Rick's Uncle Tom.

French Casino showgirls strut their stuff.

CHAPTER III
Return to Springfield
Girl Goes Ape!

In 1966 I returned to the Ozark Empire Fair. This time I was the caretaker answering people's questions. No, I hadn't wrangled a job at that two-headed cow show I saw in 1953. I was showing "Bozo the Giant Steer." (I'll tell you a little secret. This wasn't the original Bozo; the first one died a few years before.)

I hauled the steer and the show equipment inside a twenty-five-foot semi-trailer that was pulled with an old International gas-powered tractor. The Army tent had been replaced by a portable 20' x 24', red-and-white barn. This display required no stakes, so it was a lot easier to set up. Also, it looked a lot neater.

Polaroid photo taken in Springfield, Missouri, the day after the fair, 1966. Rick posed beside the International, with the ready-to-load giant steer peeking around the back of the trailer.

During the fair, I slept on a cot in the back of the trailer. Even after a thorough cleaning, the vehicle had a noticeable cow odor, but I grew used to it.

A steady line of customers waited daily to see Bozo. On one day alone, over twelve thousand people passed through the show, making it one of the busiest days I ever experienced at the fair.

"Walk all the way around him, see him from every angle. Keep the line moving so your friends and neighbors will get the opportunity to see Bozo," I called out hour after hour. I put in a long day, but I was well rewarded for my labor!

One show on the carnival midway that impressed me was a Girl-to-Gorilla illusion. (Century 21 Shows provided the carnival that year.) Behind the bally platform, lined in real bamboo, the front was painted to look like a jungle. Colorful banners displayed fanciful images of a voluptuous woman being transformed into a gorilla.

The talker was dressed in a Frank "Bring-'Em-Back-Alive" Buck African safari outfit, with khaki riding pants and shirt, brown knee-high leather boots, pith helmet, and bullwhip. He introduced the "princess" who was paraded on stage in a teensy-weensy, leopard-skin bikini. The talker explained that an evil witch doctor had put a spell on the princess, *"which will cause her to undergo a most unusual transformation that you will be able to witness firsthand"* on the inside.

"She will grow the long, coarse hair of the gorilla, all-l-l over her lovely body," he continued while slowly running his finger down the curves of her supple body. *"And right before your very eyes, her lovely body will put on an additional three hundred ugly gorilla pounds."*

Paying customers witnessed the princess locked and chained in a steel cage on the rear end of a truck that was backed into the tent. There were no seats, this show was standing room only. The lights were turned off, and Olatunji's recording of "Drums of Passion" started to play. As the muted lights in the cage brightened, the princess started her transformation.

"Gorilla-gorilla-gorilla," the talker barked into the microphone over the recorded drum music.

The scene reminded me of Lon Chaney's movie transformation into the wolf-man, except this was live! In only a few moments, the princess began her metamorphosis, slowly growing hair over her entire body. As the lights brightened all the way, a huge, hairy gorilla stood in her place, roaring and rattling the bars of the cage.

"Please, stand back, folks. I'm not sure we can contain him," the showman yelled as he cracked his whip.

Banner from a Girl to Gorilla illusion.

Omigod! At this point, with a great deal of commotion, the cage door flew open and a huge gorilla burst onto the stage. A loud siren went off at the same time, adding to the confusion. The screaming spectators jumped back from the huge ape towering above them and stampeded toward the exit. (As the gorilla "escaped," one of the employees opened a flap to the exit, showing everyone the way out.)

In minutes, the tent cleared and the performers were ready for another show. Of course, the sight of people running and screaming from the tent always helped draw a large tip for the next bally.

Now most people who saw the show probably knew it wasn't a real gorilla, just a guy in a monkey suit. But jeepers creepers, it was pitch-dark in there, and we were all packed inside a musty tent on the back-end of the carnival with people running and screaming and sirens blaring, and I knew darned well, I didn't want that gorilla to get hold of me, even if it wasn't real!

Girl Goes Ape!

A banner line from a Girl to Gorilla illusion that was on the road in 1992. The basic mechanics for this illusion have been around since the turn of the century.

CHAPTER IV
The Iceman
Preserved Forever in a Coffin of Ice!

I met Frank Hansen, wearing his trademark suit and tie, in 1967 at the Heart of Illinois Fair in Peoria. Born in Alma, Michigan, in 1922, and after retiring from the Air Force, he had broken into the carnival business to display his "Siberskoye Creature," a near-human, missing-link, Bigfoot-like creature inside a block of ice.

The six-foot-tall creature, except for its face, feet, and palms, was covered with dark-colored coarse hair resembling the hair of a bear or an ape. The hands and feet appeared human but disproportionately large. And the creature's left arm revealed a compound fracture along with a little blood in the ice near the wound. Nice touch! In addition, the opaque quality of the ice helped create an illusion and prevented fairgoers from inspecting the creature too closely.

Frank had installed wood paneling in his semi-trailer with plush red carpeting, chrome handrails, and a custom-built freezer. He lit up the side of each step leading into the exhibit like you might see at an airport. The appearance of his museum-like trailer lent credence and drama to the display, "The Siberskoye Creature frozen and preserved forever in a coffin of ice."

Frank claimed (one of many versions he told, because the story evolved with time) the Iceman was found floating by Japanese whalers inside a 6,000-pound block of ice in the Sea of Okhotsk, in eastern Siberia. The whalers then sold it to a "dealer of the unusual" in Hong Kong, who in turn sold it to a "well-known multimillionaire who has connections to the movie business in California."

Frank told me, "The owner likes to collect things that are rare, something that no one else has."

The "owner" supposedly leased the creature to Frank. All of his press interviews were deadly serious, and written up that way in newspapers, magazines, and scientific journals. The Smithsonian even asked to examine the creature in 1968 after two scientists, Ivan Sanderson and Bernard Hevuelmans, examined and photographed it for two days at Frank's place. Both men accepted the creature at face value, believing they had discovered a true, unknown hominid.

Hevuelmans' article was published in the *Bulletin of the Royal Institute of Natural Sciences of Belgium* in February 1969, entitled "Notice on a Specimen Preserved in Ice of an Unknown Form of Living Hominid: *Homo Pongoides*." Sanderson's article was entitled "The Missing Link?" and published in *Argosy* Magazine in May 1969.

I loved the show, and right then and there I wanted one. I asked Frank who built the creature. He seemed annoyed by the tone of my questions. Of course, he said it was real. After all, here was Frank, with an exhibit he paid really big bucks to build and present as a legitimate exhibit, being grilled by an eighteen-year-old kid—who looks sixteen.

Needless to say, we didn't hit it off too well at our first meeting. Anyway, I told him I was going to build a creature too!

Preliminary sketch for Rick's "Missing Link" creature.

The head of Rick's creature revealing the dead-flesh color of the latex.

In 1969, with the help of artist friend Dale Kuiper, I set out to build a creature while attending the University of Wisconsin in Green Bay. We placed Jim Dombrowski, one of Dale's friends, in plaster of Paris at his art studio/apartment above the Bay Theater. After shaving his body, we rubbed Vaseline over him, positioned him face-up, pushed the sand around him and poured the top half of our plaster mold.

We removed the 75-pound mold from atop him, turned it over, positioned him on his stomach, and poured the other half. Well, our volunteer became very uncomfortable from the heat generated as the plaster set up, plus it was difficult for Jim to breathe! However, he didn't die, so we put the two molds together and poured a positive cast inside them.

We bought 30 pounds of Plasticine modeling clay in Chicago (an eventful trip, I might add), sculpting it over the plaster cast and, in the process, created veins and pores. We wound up making several molds before we had the actual latex model. The latex naturally gave the skin a yellowish-sickly color, blue tint was added to the veins to give them a realistic look, and we took painstaking care to put the hair in right, even to the point of putting in the hairs one or two at a time.

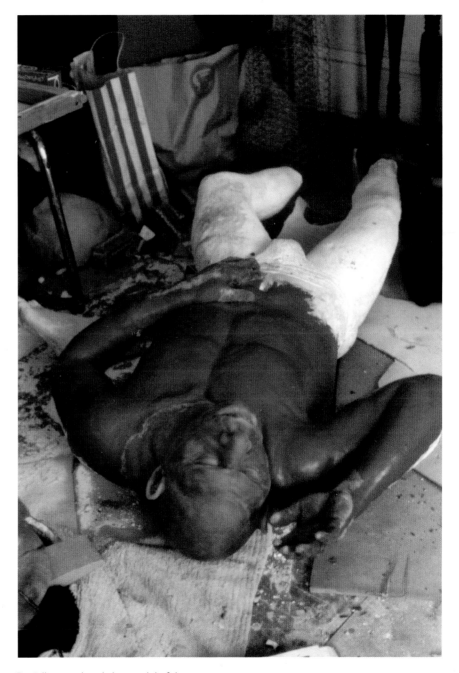

Partially completed clay model of the creature.

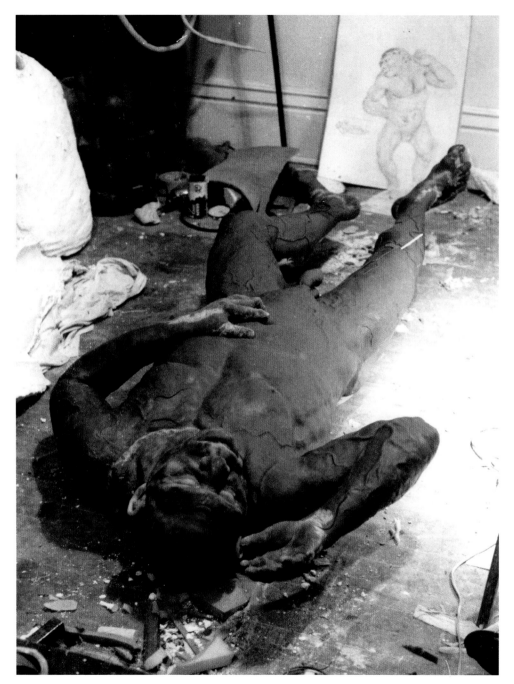

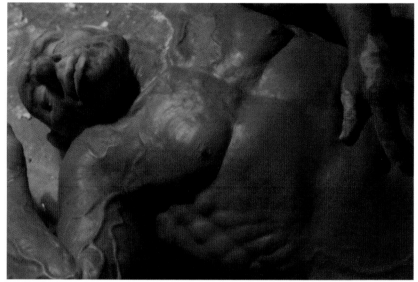

Close-up of creature.

Though I wasn't completely satisfied, our creature turned out nicely. Dale moved to Hollywood, California, shortly thereafter and worked as a movie makeup artist for *The Howling* and *Caveman*.

The finished clay model of Rick's creature with veins showing through the skin before it was cast in latex and hairs were implanted, 1969.

Dale Kuiper working on Rick's creature, 1969.

Meanwhile, Frank splashed onto the front pages of newspapers across America. Upon reentering the U.S. after a summer tour of Canada with the Iceman, American officials stopped him at the border and wouldn't let him across unless he produced a death certificate for the Iceman. Frank could only get back into the U.S. after Minnesota Senator Walter Mondale intervened and helped him clear customs. Oh yeah, Frank always made headlines.

The next time I ran into Frank was at a county fair in Wisconsin during the early 1970s. His Iceman show-trailer had been converted into a cryogenics show, and he claimed that the exhibit contained the frozen body of a wealthy lady whose dying wish was to be frozen. Supposedly, she would be brought to life in the future when science advanced enough to revive her.

Frank reportedly leased her for the display and kept her body frozen using liquid nitrogen. Uh-oh, here we go again, just like the Iceman. To illustrate the power of the freezing liquid, Frank blew up a red balloon and put it in the nitrogen, where it shriveled up. Then he removed the balloon, and the natural warmth caused it to re-inflate.

He then put a live goldfish in the nitrogen, freezing the fish solid, just like the lady. Once he removed the goldfish and put it back into the fishbowl, it revived and started swimming around. One more thing, as he talked about the cryo display, he bounced a small red ball over and over. At the end of his spiel, he put the ball into the liquid nitrogen. Then he removed the ball, "accidentally" dropping it, which caused it to shatter on the floor.

A real attention getter!

Frank explained that he had reframed the Iceman exhibit so it could fit inside shopping malls and asked me if I would be interested in showing it. Well, I was pretty busy with my own shows, so I turned him down respectfully.

In May 2002 I had not seen Frank for a while, so I decided to get back in touch with him. I couldn't find a Frank D. Hansen in the phone listings, so I figured I would start calling all the Hansen listings, one by one.

The very first one I called, a man answered, "Hansen residence."

"Hello, I'm looking for Frank Hansen." I inquired. "He used to show a 'Creature in Ice' at county fairs back in the late 1960s. Do you know him?"

"The owner took the creature back to California long ago," the voice replied. "I'm not in the business any more and it's all water under the bridge as far as I'm concerned."

Wow, my first call and I have Frank on the phone! And he's still telling the same old story after 35 years!

"Frank, this is Rick West, you know I really love that old creature display. The ice was the key that really made it work. The exhibit was just great; people are still talking about it."

Frank began to warm up. He told me he had a lot of pictures and newspaper clippings regarding the creature but would have to find them.

Four months later, while I was on the road, my inquiry paid off. Frank called to say he had some memorabilia I might be interested in, including the Iceman.

This was amazing! I made plans to visit him as soon as I finished my summer tour.

I headed for Minnesota on October 30, 2002, to rendezvous with Frank. Everything was running smoothly until I reached the southern Illinois border, six hundred miles from home. The diesel engine in my

Chevy one-ton crew-cab started acting up. It would shut off unexpectedly as I was driving. Not much fun at night on the interstate. I limped into Marion, Illinois, arriving at 6:00 A.M. and located the Chevrolet dealership. I unhitched my 32-foot trailer in the parking lot and waited for the dealership to open. The best-laid plans never go as smoothly as we expect. I was stuck in Marion for two anxious days waiting for an injection pump they had to order. What could I do, I called Frank to let him know I'd be running a couple days late. He said he had been talking with his wife just that morning and they wondered when I would get there. Of course, the repairs took longer than expected but I finally got the truck back and hit the road, seven hundred miles to go.

When I got to Winona, I pulled into the Fleet Farm parking lot and called Frank. He arrived twenty minutes later, and he led me to the rundown warehouse where his old carnival stuff was stored. I waited impatiently as Frank fumbled with the door lock. Finally, he was able to get it unlocked. As we entered, I saw the creature exhibit stored to one side.

Frank Hansen's original creature coffin/freezer in a southern Minnesota warehouse, November 2002. The display was sold as scrap metal following Frank's death.

This wasn't the original exhibit in the semi-trailer. This was the exhibit that he built to show in shopping malls. I was anxious to see the creature. What would it look like after thirty-plus years? And what would it look like without being encased in ice?

Unable to wait any longer, I grabbed my camera and notebook, and climbed the steps leading to the creature as Frank plugged in the lights. To see the creature without its ice covering was a little anticlimactic.

Iceman without the ice, 2002. Condensation on the inside of the glass hindered taking photographs with greater detail. Mold had darkened the facial features.

The creature looked like a model, although a good one, without the ice. The exhibit was in disrepair, the metal was rusted, the chrome was pitted, the carpet needed to be replaced, the refrigeration unit didn't work, the signs needed to be repainted, the 8-track sound system was obsolete, and last—but not least—the creature needed work.

But here it was, in the flesh, as they say, "The World Famous Siberskoye Creature," sitting in a dark, cluttered warehouse in a small town in southern Minnesota, where it had been gathering dust for the last twenty years. The remnants of ice that used to encase the creature melted long ago; the creature lay in a couple of inches of rusty water in its original coffin/freezer.

Considering it was over 35 years old and had sat around for the last 20 years, the creature looked pretty good. But it seemed hard to believe the creature sitting in this old warehouse caused all the media ballyhoo it did in the late 1960s.

I asked Frank lots of questions, and he told me Howard Ball designed and began to build the creature in 1967. After Howard and Frank had a falling out, two other make-up artists finished the work. Then wax figure artists Pete and Mary Corrall put the hairs in the creature. (It looked like they used black bear hair.) The creature was encased in a block of ice at a freezer plant in California and then lowered using nylon straps into the coffin that had been its home since 1967.

The Iceman's feet. The nylon straps used to lower the original block of ice into the freezer/coffin are still visible, 2002.

A sign from Frank's Iceman display.

I said, "Frank, the most interesting story is not the one you created about the creature's origin, but the true story of how you came up with the whole Iceman idea."

I'm a little surprised that Frank answered without any hesitation or reluctance. I thought he still might want to repeat the old story about the mysterious California owner, but he didn't.

"I was at a fair," he said. "I think it may have been the Minnesota State Fair and saw a show that was making a lot of money. They had a long line but when the people came out you could see they were really disappointed."

"Do you remember what show it was?" I asked.

"I can't remember, Rick."

I phrased the question differently. "Can you remember what type of show it was?"

"I just can't remember," Frank replied.

"So you see this sideshow that is making a lot of money," I reminded him.

"Yeah," Frank said, "and I think I could do it better. I'll give them something to talk about when they leave my show! There was a lot of interest in the Missing Link and Bigfoot at the time. I went out to California where I met Bud Westmore, who was working for Universal Studios' makeup department.

"He told me about Howard Ball. I met with Howard, who had done some work for Disney, and told him what I wanted, leaving out the carnival part, of course." Frank's eyes sparkled as he stood beside the freezer remembering those heady days in the late '60s when everyone was talking about his "Creature in Ice."

Rick and Frank at the Iceman Exhibit, 2002.

"Where was the first spot you played with the Creature?" I asked.

Frank thought for a minute. "I can't remember any more." He was having considerable trouble remembering details, names, even words. I was puzzled.

I asked him about the 1970 *Saga* Magazine article in which he said he shot the creature while hunting in Minnesota.

"I was just trying to keep the creature in the news," he replied matter-of-factly.

"Can you remember the biggest day you ever had showing the Iceman?" I asked.

"I don't remember, but it had to be big," he said. "They would stand in line all day to get a look at the creature. Sometimes the mall would be closing for the night, and we would still have a line. The maintenance people really hated how late we held them up."

I changed the subject. "How much are you going to ask for the creature exhibit?"

"It's a gold mine, you know," he replied. "I don't want to scare you off, but I won't be selling it for pennies. It won't be here long. People will stand in line all day to get a look at it. How much are you willing to offer for it?"

"How much do you want for it?" I asked again.

"Make me an offer and I will consider it," he replied.

Frank did not seem to have a price in mind, so I told Frank I would give it some thought. At this point, it occurred to me that at some future date I might discover that he gave the creature away, which was exactly what he did with the cryogenics display.

I asked a lot of other questions, but Frank could not remember many of the details. I persisted until Frank looked down for a moment, then looking me squarely in the eye, he said, "You can just make it up if you want, Rick."

What a revelation! This was really important. Frank had just given me permission to make up stories about the Iceman just as he had done for so long. He liked to tell stories. He didn't think the real story was all that important. And his show was incredible! Frank created one of the best shows I had ever seen!

Frank standing on his exhibit, reminiscing about the Iceman a few months before his death, November 2002. This was the last time Rick saw him.

How ironic was it that Frank could no longer remember the details of the Iceman story? After all the years of telling wonderful stories about the Iceman, and he told some great ones, Frank couldn't remember the true stories behind his "World Famous Siberskoye Creature, preserved forever in a coffin of ice!"

Two things made the "Creature in Ice" a great show. One was the story that Frank created to explain the Iceman's discovery, which made him the caretaker, not the owner. The other element was the twenty-five hundred pounds of ice that encased the creature.

Ice made the whole thing believable. Without the ice, it would have been just another creature show on the carnival midway. With the ice—key to creating the illusion—the show reflected Frank's genius.

A few months after my visit, Frank was admitted to the hospital suffering from dementia. I would not get to speak to Frank again; he died March 23, 2003.

Frank's death brought down the final curtain on his "World Famous Siberskoye Creature."

Rick and Frank in front of the Iceman display. This is the display Frank framed to play shopping malls.

Frank Hansen's defrosted 35-year-old "World Famous Creature in Ice," 2002.

CHAPTER V
Octopus, Whales, and Monster Trucks
Weird and Wild Walk-Throughs!

I got the chance to play the Calgary Stampede in Alberta the first time I toured Canada. I was fifteen years old that summer and working for my Uncle Tom. At Calgary we met a guy from California who had created an amazing octopus exhibit. He showcased his eight-armed monster inside a round eight-foot-diameter propane tank painted metallic green. Holes were cut in the tank and brass portholes installed around the circumference through which you could view the sea creature. The entire display was mounted on a flatbed trailer, which contained a walkway around the tank and what appeared to be a papier-mâché octopus mounted on a pole on top of the tank.

The show owner/operator told us he had found an enormous octopus measuring twelve feet across its tentacles washed up on a beach in California. He hauled the creature home and made a cast and model of it using latex rubber. He bought a huge tank and installed pneumatics to animate the latex octopus so it would move up and down. The tank was filled with water and the pneumatics activated. As the creature moved, air bubbles floated up through the water and caused the tentacles to reach out toward the portholes, making it appear very lifelike.

After a typical curiosity-seeker viewed the octopus, he might ask what the creature ate. After the owner told them it was animated, the spectator would respond, "I know that, but what does it eat?"

Like I said, it appeared to be very lifelike.

The Octopus Show after Jimmy Allen mounted the eight-foot tank in a show-front trailer, Lake County Fair, Grayslake, Illinois.

Jimmy Allen, who toured the fair circuit with a house that was carved from a giant redwood log, bought the Octopus Show in the 1970s and mounted the tank in a semi-trailer. Before he rebuilt the exhibit, you could see the tank from anywhere—around the front, side, and back—but once Jimmy changed it you could only view it from the front. The change weakened the show. And last I heard, after Jimmy died, the octopus wound up stored in a warehouse in Chicago. Jimmy's daughter, Jamie Allen, remains in the business and still shows the Redwood Log House, the nicest of four or five redwood log homes that toured America over the years.

Speaking of sea life, Little Irvy the Whale was one of the most beautiful shows on the circuit. When I say beautiful, I am talking about the exhibit, not the whale. After years spent in a refrigerated trailer, the frozen whale was, ahem, how should I put it, far from beautiful.

The twenty-ton, thirty-eight-foot Pacific sperm whale was shown in a semi-tractor trailer rig. Jerry "Tyrone" Malone, a balding used-car salesman from Visalia, California, invested a great deal of time and borrowed money into the whale project.

First, he had to secure a permit from the federal government, no easy task. He needed to figure out how to freeze a 20-ton whale. You just can't stop by your local cryogenics lab. And finally, Jerry required some conveyance in which to haul it. Malone's ingenuity solved all these problems.

Jamie Allen's Redwood Log House at the Florida State Fair.

Detail of Jamie Allen's Log House.

He purchased a 1967 Kenworth truck and trailer, and painted them baby blue with dark blue pinstripes. After customizing the trailer into the whale's new mobile home, the rig dripped chrome: chrome wheels, chrome rails, a chrome radiator shroud, and chrome mirrors. He installed whitewall tires and even placed a small chrome whale ornament on the radiator cap. He named the flashy 18-wheeler "Old Blue." Next, Jerry discovered what it took to freeze an oceanic giant: one week and 80,000 gallons of liquid nitrogen.

The show took up about sixty-five feet of midway frontage, an impressive display. And it worked! People paid thirty-five cents for a peek at the whale. Once they finally got inside, they expressed surprise it was frozen. But what were these people thinking? That someone could keep a thirty-eight-foot whale alive inside a semi-trailer?

The tradition of the pay-to-view whale exhibit dates back to at least P.T. Barnum's display of an iced whale corpse at his American Museum in New York.

Jerry Malone's frozen Whale Exhibit was pulled by a 1967 custom Kenworth named "Old Blue."

"Little Irvy" at the Lethbridge Exhibition & Stampede Days in Lethbridge, Alberta, Canada, 1971.

"Boss Truck," a 1971, 20,000-pound, 540-horsepower Kenworth, being unloaded from its specially built hauler named "Mama Truck."

When Jerry took the truck out on exhibition, he hauled it on another custom-built Kenworth that he called the "Mama Truck." Rick Owens, who worked for Jerry, kept the Boss Truck running all day, revving it up occasionally. Whenever he hit the Jake Brake, the noise attracted quite a crowd.

Billed as the $100,000 Show Truck, the "Boss Truck of America" set a land-speed record of 114 miles per hour at the Bonneville Salt Flats, Utah.

Later, after learning folks liked to look at his truck as much as the frozen cetacean cadaver, Jerry, now billed as the "daredevil diesel driver," built "Boss Truck of America." This souped-up 20,000-pound Kenworth semi-tractor put out an amazing 540 horsepower. He took the truck to the Bonneville Salt Flats in the early 1970s and set a land speed record, 114 mph, in the stock diesel class. He then paid big bucks to have it custom-painted and the fifth wheel gold-plated.

Rick displayed the Creature Show at Texas shopping centers, 1979.

After securing a sponsorship from Bandag Retreads, Jerry hit the big time with his Bandag Diesel Racing Team. He built several more show trucks including the 1,300-horsepower "Super Boss," the "Bandag Bandit" and the wheel-standing "Defiance." He performed in truck shows, burnouts, and exhibits all over the USA, Canada, Europe, and Australia. On his return from the land down under, Jerry brought back a genuine eighteen-foot great white shark and put it on display in a refrigerated trailer, just like Little Irvy.

Rick Owens ran Jerry's Whale Show as well as a "What is It?" exhibit, which I bought from them. When I went out to California to pick it up, I met Rick in Visalia and we went over to Jerry's office to finalize the purchase. After our meeting, he showed me through the shop where they were building another show truck and "Papa Truck." I reframed the "What is It?" exhibit, presented it as a Bigfoot Creature, and showed it around the country for several years before selling it back to Rick in 1984.

Removing the glass from the Creature's coffin so the interior could be refurbished.

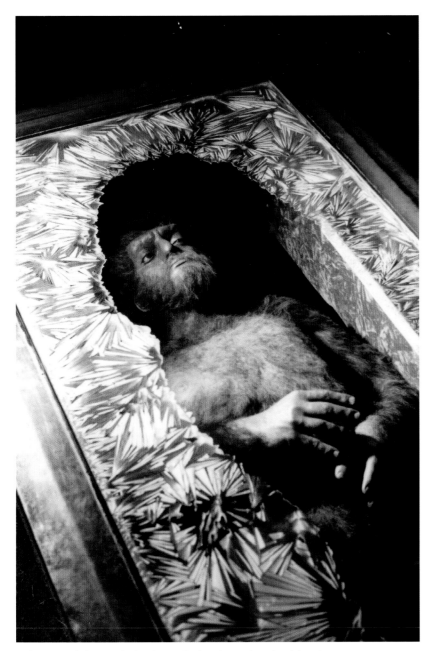

Rick acquired chemicals that he applied to the underside of the glass, creating the artificial ice/frost illusion.

Tyrone Malone, the Daredevil Diesel Driver's "Super Boss" exhibition truck. The custom diesel dragster was powered by a V-12 Detroit Diesel that produced 1,300 horsepower. It set a 144 mile-per-hour land-speed record at the Bonneville Salt Flats, Utah.

In January 1997, while in Phoenix to discuss his multimillion-dollar plans to build a "Truckers Hall of Fame" disaster struck. According to the Arizona State Patrol, Jerry fell asleep behind the wheel, lost control of his vehicle and ironically crashed into a fellow trucker. The tragedy abruptly ended the life and illustrious thirty-year career of the "Daredevil Diesel Driver."

Another custom built hauler named the "Papa Truck" under construction, 1978.

See ya' down the road!

Rick with Malone's "Super Boss" truck in Visalia, California.

CHAPTER VI
Hitler's Armor-Plated Limousine
Art of the Ding!

I first met Pete Sevich in Canada in 1963 at the Red River Exhibition in Winnipeg, Manitoba. Pete, a no-nonsense guy with an off-center nose, looked German, a convenient twist of fate for someone exhibiting Adolf Hitler's 1943 armor-plated Mercedes-Benz limousine.

The black 9,500-pound limo had an aluminum body with inch-and-a-half-thick bulletproof windows. One window was cracked and pitted from a gunshot, but the bullet had not penetrated the glass. A four-inch hole had been cut through the rear quarter panel so people could see and touch the armor plating.

Hitler's 1943 armor-plated Mercedes-Benz, weight 9,500 lbs., length 19' 5", fuel capacity 70 gallons, fuel economy 3 miles per gallon, top speed 135 mph, glass 1¼-inch thick, reportedly captured May 7, 1945.

Two gas tanks and two distributors were installed, so if one quit, the engine kept running. Supposedly, the tires were bulletproof, too (although I remember they were nearly flat).

The bulletproof limousine was shown in a walk-through semi-trailer that opened in the front with steps leading up into the display. Documentation displayed out front showed the car belonged to Adolf Hitler and disclosed the date of import into the U.S. Pete also displayed many Nazi items, including flags, uniforms, and daggers. He either charged twenty-five cents admission or operated it as a ding.

When a show operator runs a ding, everyone is invited to come in as if the exhibit were free.

Therefore, typical fairgoers thought, "This sounds great. Let's get in line."

What visitors might fail to notice was a small inconspicuous sign, "This display is run on donations. Thank you very much."

For those who did see the sign, a typical reaction was, "We don't have to pay if it's a donation, right?"

Well, after viewing the car, feeling the armor plating and the thickness of the windows, visitors would approach the exit where Pete stood with his hand out. Apparently everyone "donated" a minimum of one dollar, because on the counter were nothing but $1 and $5 bills. In order not to look like a cheapskate, out comes a buck!

The Hitler Bulletproof Car display.

Hitler Car Exhibit, complimentary admission ticket.

Here's what people didn't know. No matter what a customer handed Pete—a dime or a quarter—he threw down a dollar, so the people still in line thought everyone was giving a dollar. The ding worked pretty sweet sometimes! It also helped if the aisleway was small, there was only one way out, and the operator of the display was in the middle of the aisle, sort of blocking a visitor's exit until he came up with a donation.

But hey, it *was* free! I would never try to beat a man at his own game. No wonder I loved the fair!

Let me digress from Pete's story for a moment. Remember when I visited Frank Hansen during the fall of 2002? While I was looking through the warehouse, I saw his "Lord's Last Supper" wax-figure exhibit sitting in one corner, which Frank used to operate as a ding, too.

He described how he bought the wax heads and hands that were used in a famous German passion play before World War II. Supposedly they were smuggled into the U.S. from Germany after the Nazi regime collapsed. Frank dickered the exhibit's previous owners down to $3,000 cash, which he peeled from a roll of bills in his pocket, for the entire lifelike set.

Next he built a walk-through trailer that had an entrance on one end with a one-way turnstile, so people could not back out once they entered. At the other end, he constructed an exit controlled by a turnstile with a foot-operated release.

If Frank didn't stand on the cable release, the turnstile wouldn't turn. Frank positioned a mirror so he could see when people were leaving the exhibit. When a customer came along who ignored the donation box, the turnstile appeared to be stuck. Frank pretended to appear nonchalant as the person pushed against it several times.

As the perplexed patron stood there trying to get the unforgiving turnstile to budge, Frank stared at the donation box and suggested, "Maybe you forgot a little something!"

The fairgoer put some money into the donation box, and the turnstile worked. It was a miracle!

"This way [using the turnstile] one person could run the show, and I didn't have to depend on help," Frank explained.

"People viewing Christ and His disciples would be so moved some would be crying, some praying. Some people were so moved they put $5 or $10 in the mooch [donation] box as they left. If they didn't put a little something in the box, I didn't trip the turnstile and they couldn't get out!"

Frank's exhibit was a strong ding-show; for one, it had the religious element, and two, Frank controlled the exit turnstile. Like all ding-shows,

sometimes the patrons needed a little encouragement to show their appreciation!

Anyway, getting back to Pete Sevich, the last time I saw Pete was at a small Ohio county fair in 1967. His son was getting ready to start college in the fall, and Pete was thinking about getting off the road and selling the Hitler limo.

Randall's Giant Horse Show.

The Randall family purchased the bulletproof limo and show trailer from Pete in 1974. Their son Charlie took the exhibit on tour, playing fairs and shopping centers. (This was the family's second grind show; they also owned "Big John the Giant Horse.")

Hitler's Armored Mercedes-Benz display at a shopping center.

They had a few lucrative years showing the car before the neo-Nazi, skinhead movement stirred up anti-Nazi sentiments. The limousine became a focal point for these explosive sentiments even though the exhibit was never pro-Nazi. The shopping centers the Randalls played began receiving phoned-in bomb threats, and they would have to shut down the exhibit and hightail it out of town. Charlie also had to deal with increasingly violent confrontations.

In desperation, they completely dropped the Hitler name and tried to exhibit the car as, "The World Famous Bulletproof Car!" Unfortunately, income dropped like a lead balloon.

With no real solution in sight, "Hitler's Bulletproof Limo" was taken off the road permanently. In 1980, the Randalls sold the car to an investor.

A large-caliber bullet hit the rear side window of Hitler's limousine, but the shot didn't penetrate the bulletproof glass. A four-inch hole was cut into the aluminum body so paying customers could feel the steel plating.
One of Adolf Hitler's limos, a Mercedes-Benz 770K parade sedan, sold for $153,000 at an auction in Arizona during 1973, the highest price paid for an auctioned car up to that time. In 2000, the Canadian War Museum in Ottawa, Ontario, considered selling its Hitler limousine, believing it would bring $20 million at auction. But a public outcry ensued, and the museum decided against putting it on the market.

Chapter VII
My Two-Headed Cow
The Cash Cow!

While working in Canada during July 1972, I came across a newspaper article about a two-headed calf born in Saskatchewan, Canada. I immediately thought back in time to when I saw a two-headed cow at my first fair when I was five years old. Without any hesitation, I made arrangements to visit the festival where the seven-week-old calf was on display.

I wasn't disappointed; it was beautiful. I could see all four brown eyes and its two mouths. Unfortunately, I had a four-month fair route to finish, so the two-headed calf would have to wait. I took a few photographs, because I could not predict how long the calf might live.

Once I finished the summer fair circuit, I was ready to move. I looked up the owner's name and address— Emile Desnoyer in Coderre, Saskatchewan—from the article, called information, and got his phone number. After getting Emile on the phone, I inquired how the calf was doing. He told me it was healthy and had gained thirty pounds.

I asked, "Are you interested in selling the calf?"

"If the price is right, eh," he replied in a heavy Canadian accent.

I didn't need any more of an invitation to start haggling, and we quickly settled on a price, twenty-five hundred dollars. I made plans for a trip to Canada.

Since it was December, I thought it might be a little cold up there. So I enclosed the back of my pickup with an aluminum camper shell, and loaded three sleeping bags along with a catalytic heater into the truck bed. That's how Wayne Bradley, my wife Teri, and I headed into Saskatchewan.

Rick's two-headed calf was born on a farm in Coderre, Saskatchewan, Canada, April 16, 1972.

The extreme cold of the 1,200-mile trip taught the three of us Wisconsin residents a thing or two—the temperature never rose above minus ten degrees during our journey. The last sixty miles were the worse. The truck and I battled an ice-covered gravel road while the relentless wind blew snow into hard-packed drifts that nearly blocked our way.

The terrain was desolate. Any kind of mechanical breakdown would put us in a life-threatening situation. We were in the midst of the treeless plains of Saskatchewan, in the middle of nowhere, with nothing for miles around, except an awful, incessant wind. All we could think about was getting out of this deep freeze.

We arrived at the Desnoyer farm late that afternoon, took a quick look at the calf and hurried to the warmth of the farmhouse. The next morning as we loaded the calf to head back to the States, the thermometer read a bone-chilling minus thirty-five degrees and the wind blew a steady forty miles an hour. The air was so cold and dry that it hurt my throat and lungs to even breathe. And I thought Wisconsin was cold!

There Goes Tradition—Mr. and Mrs. Rick West exchange the traditional kiss following their wedding before County Judge Clarence Nier Monday as witnesses Prof. and Mrs. Robert Fritz look on. The kiss was the only wedding tradition left in the ceremony which featured the gals dressed in pantsuits because that's the way the bride wanted it. (Story Page A-8)

(Press-Gazette Photo)

Rick and Teri were married in 1969, the year an American landed on the moon and a music festival in Woodstock jammed roads in New York state. The bride sported a pants outfit, and Rick wore a fringed leather jacket that set off his shoulder-length hair. The wedding made the front page of the Green Bay Press-Gazette with the headline, "There Goes Tradition." (Unfortunately, their marriage ended in 1984.)

Rick and his two-headed wonder dreaming of warmer weather.

I tied a red bandana over my mouth to help warm the frigid air before it reached my lungs. Wayne, Teri, and I wrapped a pink blanket around the calf, securing it with binder twine.

The 1972 Chevy pickup cranked slowly, and I thought the engine was never going to start. The truck had sat outside overnight, and it seemed logical, to me at least, that these extreme temperatures had nearly solidified the engine oil.

"Rrr-rr-rr-rr," a few seconds of silence, "rrr-rr-rr," I pumped the throttle as the engine continued to crank slowly.

"Please, let this darn thing start so we can get out of here," I prayed silently.

I didn't think anything good was going to happen, but the engine finally started. Next I noticed the heat from our bodies caused quarter-inch-thick frost to form on the inside of the windows. To look out of the truck, we had to scrape the ice from inside.

Even with an ice-scraper and the defroster running full blast, the frosted windows never completely cleared, but at least we were headed south. We drove all day and some of the night until we located a gas station near the U.S.–Canada border.

I looked at the station's two repair bays and figured the temperature inside had to be considerably warmer than the icebox surrounding my truck. A teenage attendant walked our way, and I asked, "Can I pull the truck into a repair bay for a few hours?"

"Well, I don't know," he replied.

The temperature was dropping again. I became concerned not only with the welfare of my wife and friend, but for the calf I was hauling. I began to realize I had some pretty interesting cargo that this boy might want to see. And the truck should start nicely after a night in a warm enclosed space.

"Hey, have ya' ever seen a two-headed calf?" I asked.

"Nope," he answered as his eyes widened. "Do you...?" He had grown so excited he couldn't finish his sentence!

"Maybe," I smiled.

He paused and walked slowly around my truck to inspect the camper top. Through the rear-view mirror, I saw him trying to peer inside.

"I'll tell you what," I called out. "If I show you a real live two-headed calf, will you let me use your repair bay?"

"You won't tell anyone, will you?" he replied.

"Of course not," I winked.

And in a couple of minutes, Wayne, Teri, and I— including my own two-headed cow—were safe and warm inside the heated repair bay.

When I got home, I started building my "Two-Headed Cow" display at the University of Wisconsin's art studio, which was housed in an old warehouse. The display consisted of a portable barn built out of three-quarter-inch conduit pipe, covered with quarter-inch plywood, painted red with white lettering.

I used an acetylene torch to braze the pipe together, which filled the art studio with a blue haze. Before I knew it, I came down with the flu—the worst case of flu I ever had—along with everyone else in the art department.

I lost twenty-five pounds and after two weeks I only weighed 110 pounds. By the time I finished brazing the display together, I had thrown up so hard and so many times I had ruptured the blood vessels in my eyes.

What I didn't know at the time was that we had chlorine poisoning. As I welded the galvanized pipe, I was creating chlorine gas, the deadly blue haze that could have killed us!

Rick's two-headed cow, "Alive and Breathing," at the Southwest Livestock Show in El Paso, Texas, 1973. Paula Ben manned the ticket box.

Everyone in the art department thought I was creating a giant metal pipe sculpture, until I started to rivet plywood on the 20-foot-square by 13-foot-high frame. Then everyone thought I was building a portable garage. Fifteen hundred rivets later, I finished the framing, threw on a couple coats of red paint, hand-lettered the front of the display, and was ready for the road.

The first spot I showed the calf, other than to the gas station attendant of course, was the Southwest Livestock Show in El Paso, Texas. Five of us—my wife Teri; my sister Vicki and her boyfriend, Dean Vanden Heuvel; friend Paula "Ben" Jacobson; and I—headed for Texas in my '72 Chevy pickup. It was a little crowded, to say the least, but everyone was up for an adventure.

Rick's two-headed heifer calf, 1972.

Rick's 1972 Chevy with Avion camper used to haul the two-headed cow to Texas.

My ten-foot Avion truck camper was situated in the bed of the pickup, and I pulled a sixteen-foot livestock trailer containing the two-headed calf and the display I built. And guess who loaned me the trailer? My Uncle Tom, of course.

After El Paso, we played a few more spots in Texas, including some shopping centers. At one particular Austin shopping center, the calf came down with pneumonia. To help fight off the infection, I gave it a shot of penicillin.

Bad move. The two-headed calf was allergic to penicillin and was dead by morning! The show was over!

49

I felt pretty bad the next morning as we tore down the display and loaded everything into the trailer, including the dead calf. I thought that if I was really good, if I really was meant to do this, I'd go ahead and show the dead two-headed calf and tell everyone she was sleeping!

Anyway, we stopped at an International House of Pancakes® to eat breakfast and discuss what to do with the dead calf. One of the customers overheard us talking, and said he would like to have it.

Great! After finishing our pancakes, we went outside to load the dead calf into the back of the guy's old Ford van. To this day, I have no idea what he did with it. For all I know, he stuffed it and put it on display as a roadside curiosity somewhere along a Texas highway.

One man's dead two-headed calf is another man's cash cow!

See Jessie the live two-headed cow. The most incredible exhibit you will ever see! Created by God, not the hand of man. She has a mouth to drink with and a mouth to eat with. Look into her four big brown eyes. She's alive, she's real. You have to see it to believe it, we didn't believe it ourselves until we saw it.

A two-headed calf postcard pitched at Rick's show.

DOLLY   The Only Live 2 Headed Cow in the World

Dolly and Rolly was a famous two-headed cow shown in the 1930s and '40s. The pitch claimed one head was female and one male.
The back of the card offered, "If you can find another like her, we will pay you $100,000."

Chapter VIII
Joe and the Cattalo
It's Showtime!

Joe Cisneroz is married to my first wife's older sister, Karen. Joe is extremely handsome, with dark brown eyes. His father was Spanish, his mother Mexican, and he inherited his good looks from both parents. Joe is a former rock musician, the bass player with Skip Arne and the Dukes who had one national hit, "Cherry Pie." Wanting to spend more time with his growing family, he quit the road and took a job with Abbott Laboratories in Waukegan, Illinois.

Every time Joe and Karen visited relatives in Green Bay, thieves would break into their Waukegan house and steal their stuff. The idea of leaving the rat race tantalized them, and they dreamed about a quiet country farm of their own.

On one of their visits, they discovered an old Victorian farmhouse with forty acres of land for sale near Denmark, Wisconsin, 17 miles south of Green Bay. He asked me to look at it with them.

As we pulled up, we noticed the farmhouse needed paint. There wasn't a speck of paint left on it, but we could tell it had been quite a showplace in its day, with etched glass panes in the doors and gingerbread decorations around the top of the porches.

After completing our inspection of the exterior, we were anxious to see what the inside looked like. As we entered the dining room we were dumbstruck! A two-foot-high pile of potatoes greeted us. I had seen a lot of unusual stuff, but the unexpected sight of a couple hundred pounds of potatoes really surprised me.

"That's impressive!" I laughed. "I wonder what sort of people store their potatoes in the dining room, Joe? Does the movie *Deliverance* come to mind?"

We walked into the kitchen. In front of the kitchen sink was a major-sized hole in the floor revealing an eight-foot drop onto the basement's

Joe and Karen's farm house as they bought it, 1973.

52

concrete floor. You might say access to the sink was a little awkward.

Joe asked, "Hey, Rick, do you think we can fix it up?"

I answered assuredly, "Yep, no problem!"

That was all the encouragement they needed. They bought the farm, Joe quit his city job, and they moved to Wisconsin, just like the TV show, *Green Acres*.

Joe and Karen stayed at Star Farm with Teri and me, while Joe and I remodeled their house five miles away. The first time we worked on it, I asked Joe to square up the hole in the kitchen floor with the skill saw.

He picked up the saw, pressed the switch to turn it on, heard the menacing whine of the saw's motor, and immediately held the saw as far from his body as his arm would reach.

"Holy shit, Rick! These things are dangerous!" he shouted.

The farmhouse after restoration.

I laughed. He laughed. Then we made up for Joe's lack of power tool experience by getting that house in livable condition within three months. A day didn't go by that we didn't work together. We had a great time. He continued making repairs, embellishing it and eventually restored it to its former glory, a beautiful Victorian farmhouse.

During the time they stayed with us, Karen became pregnant. I was excited. I had raised puppies, kittens, and hamsters. I had seen cows and horses give birth and baby birds hatch, but I had never had the opportunity to witness a live human birth. Finally I was going to see it.

Days and months went by. Finally, one morning at 3 A.M., Joe phoned with the words, "It's time! Get over here!"

Karen had gone into labor. We lived fairly close, so it wasn't a long or difficult drive. But as Teri and I got into the truck, snow was falling heavily and once we got on the road, I had to negotiate foot-high snowdrifts.

Normally, a home delivery with an attending physician isn't a big deal. After all, Joe and Karen only lived 17 miles from town. Unfortunately, the gathering winter storm delayed the doctor. After at least an hour of anxious waiting, he finally arrived.

We left him alone with Karen for a few minutes. After a brief examination, he called us back and declared, "False labor!"

The doctor gave Karen an injection to relax her. I thought, "False labor! Darn, I might as well go to work. Got up at 3 o'clock in the morning for nothing."

I called a wrecker to pull my truck through the snowdrifts in their quarter-mile-long driveway. That was the only way I could get to the feed mill where I worked during the off-season. Teri stayed with Joe and Karen.

When I got home from work, Teri was not home so I called Joe and Karen's place. Joe answered.

"Hey, it's me," I said. "How's it going?"

"The baby's been born," Joe replied matter-of-factly.

"Yeah, yeah, right!" I said sarcastically.

"No, really," Joe insisted.

I paused for a moment, trying to understand how such an event could happen without me. "Really? The baby's been born?"

"Yeah!" he said.

Born? I thought he was kidding. I planned to be there at the moment of birth. I had been waiting nine months for this. Couldn't Karen have waited for me to get home?

I headed over to Joe and Karen's farm. Once there, I learned that not long after I left, Karen went into labor for real. The doctor didn't make it back to the farm in time, so Joe performed the delivery. Teri offered a great deal of moral support I know, but Joe did what he had to do, even managing to cut and tie the umbilical cord.

Joe and Teri finished telling me what happened. Now it was time to go upstairs and see mother and baby. I was a little nervous, because anyone who knows me can testify I'm not a big baby fan.

Baby animals are cute. Baby kittens, baby puppies, adorable! But baby humans are not that attractive, unless the babies have two heads or some other outstanding anomaly. So imagine my astonishment when I discovered this was the most beautiful baby that had ever been born, and I think I'm being objective here.

Joe and Karen's newborn daughter, Anna, was no wrinkled, pink, crying, hairless prune. Anna was born with smooth, olive skin and a full head of soft, black baby hair. Her skin was perfectly smooth, clean, with no blood or anything disgusting. And a full head of hair! That's a real plus!

Not only that, she didn't cry! There was something miraculous about this baby's birth. Okay, there was the emotional attachment of Karen being family and all, but this was the most beautiful baby I had ever seen.

Hurry, hurry, hurry! See the most beautiful baby ever born to man! Alive and real, on the inside. Get your ticket and go now!

Anna Cisneroz, 1977.

Billie, the half-Hereford, half-bison cattalo.

For a moment, I thought about asking Karen if she would let me show Anna at the fairs. But I figured, nah, this was *not* a good time for a joke. Karen had been through a rough couple of days and a doctor's false labor diagnosis. I didn't think she felt like joking.

In the spring, I put together a grind show that Joe and I would exhibit during the fair season. Did I forget to mention Joe was going on the road as my partner? As our feature attraction I bought a rust-colored cattalo, a cross between an American bison bull and a Hereford cow. The cattalo looked a lot like a buffalo, but had a white face and beard.

Our first spot was the Heart of Illinois Fair in Peoria, but our location was terrible: away from the main traffic flow with a telephone pole smack-dab in the middle of the doorway. A real "doniker" (carnival slang for "bad") location, if ever there was one. Folks had to walk around the pole just to come inside! We didn't make any money, but we tried to enjoy the fair.

Bobby Berosini, a well-known Hollywood animal trainer, was displaying his apes, gorillas, chimpanzees, and orangutans at this fair. And his show was set up near mine. (His orangutan, Clyde, performed in the movie, *Every Which Way But Loose*, with Clint Eastwood.)

I walked over with Joe to see the apes, and something strange happened. The moment Joe walked in, one of the orangutans noticed him and began to stare. As Joe eased closer to the cages, the orangutan threw a fit. The primate tried to threaten him by banging on the bars and throwing food against the glass. We found it astonishing that every time Joe came back, the orangutan picked him out of the crowd—even if there were thirty people there—and went bananas.

Now the ape may not have liked Joe, but Bobby Berosini's wife did. She could never spend enough time at my Cattalo Show. Joe is one of those men that some might call "blessed" or "cursed," depending on the situation. Much to Karen's dismay, women are attracted to him like bees to nectar.

Whenever I go out with him to a restaurant, as soon as the waitress appears to take our order, I become invisible. Women are completely mesmerized when they talk to Joe.

He has a great sense of humor too. I've seen him glance at a family in a restaurant, eyeball the wife, mull over the situation, and then ask the woman's husband straight-faced, "How much for the woman and children?"

Maybe it's his Spanish/Mexican heritage, dark brown eyes, warm smile or sense of humor, but I always believed there was more than that... let's just call it a *gift*. Joe is daredevil handsome.

The only other time I observed this kind of charisma was back in college. Whenever Grif Johnson, a friend of mine at the University of Wisconsin in Green Bay, walked into a room crowded with people, everyone would stop to look at him. He had their full attention. It was the most amazing thing to witness time after time.

But when Grif got married, the magic went away. It just left! He could walk into that same room of people, and this time no one would pay any attention to him. He didn't look any different, but the magic, whatever *it* was, had gone.

I was dumbfounded. It was like God took *it* away. I asked Grif what happened, but he had no explanation for the loss. He wasn't even aware exactly when the magic left, but I knew.

Anyway, I was talking about Joe. Joe still has the gift. And since show people have a highly developed appreciation for such gifts, you can see why Berosini's buxom showgirl wife asked Joe to come over daily and help her with one thing or another.

I must say this about Joe. Joe was a true gentleman; he never refused to help her.

Before the summer was over we took the cattalo home and re-lettered the show-barn front so we could exhibit Hercules, a giant horse that my cousin Wayne bought. Hercules was pretty doggoned big, sorrel with a blond mane and tail, tipping the scales at 2,500 pounds.

While driving from the fair in Topeka to the Kansas State Fair in Hutchinson, I felt the horse lie down in the trailer. This wasn't normal behavior for a horse in transit. Something unusual must have happened, so I pulled over on the shoulder of the highway.

Hercules was lying almost flat. He looked pretty sick, was breathing heavily and covered with sweat. Realizing he was stressed, we had to get him up and out of the trailer as fast as possible.

I tried to get him up. Whether there wasn't enough room or some other reason, Hercules just thrashed about. Either he wasn't cooperating or he couldn't get up. I knew that Joe and I couldn't unload him by the side of the highway. So we got back into the truck and looked for a suitable place to pull off.

Twenty minutes later, I spotted an empty rodeo arena. I pulled in, and while Joe looked for a pay phone to call a veterinarian, I tried to figure out what to do.

The two of us would not be able to slide a horse this size out of the trailer. It was hot and humid outside, and Hercules looked like he was ready to die. This was an emergency!

I waited for Joe to come back, and told him my plan. I positioned the truck at the foot of a slight hill, and drove two of the portable barn's two-foot steel tent stakes into the ground until only six inches were sticking out. I grabbed hold of a three-quarter-inch nylon rope, tied one end to the stakes and the other end to the horse's hind feet.

Joe and I broke apart a bale of straw for the horse to land on. (The distance from the floor of the trailer to the ground underneath was about 16 inches.) I got in the truck and rapidly popped the clutch two or three times, jerking the truck and trailer up the hill. This caused the rope to tighten, pulling the ailing horse out the back door.

Hercules landed on the straw uninjured. My plan was working. We tied a rope around his neck, and pulled it at such an angle that his head came up. Hercules spread out his front feet, and we kept pulling on the rope. By the time the vet arrived, the horse was standing.

Our accomplishment was short-lived. The vet told us our horse had contracted tetanus. For the next few weeks, we exhibited the horse, although the tetanus caused him to become very stiff.

Hercules could not put his head down to eat. Each day and night, we held his feed and water tubs up for him and administered the medicine the vet had given us. Because he was too weak to handle a rider, Joe and I took turns trotting Hercules after we closed at night, not getting to bed until 2 or 3 a.m.

Horses rarely recover from tetanus, but I'm proud to say that in one month we had him moving and eating regularly. We saved Hercules by continuing to show him, which allowed us to be with him every minute of every day.

I told Joe, "You always have to get to the fair, no matter what!"

It didn't matter if you had a flat tire, broke an axle on the trailer or were sick, you still had to get to the fair and set up. Hey, this is show business, and the next spot just might be the Big One!

We had our most profitable fair of the summer at Hutchinson. And we saw Hoyt Axton and the Pointer Sisters perform in the grandstand. After the concert, I was able to visit with Hoyt back at his tour bus.

Joe received a real initiation into the carnival business our first year together. For several years thereafter, he exhibited one of my giant horses at shopping centers and county fairs around the country.

In 1980, Joe and Karen sold their Denmark, Wisconsin farm to the Catholic Church, which turned it into a religious retreat. The old silo and granary were converted into guest lodgings, and the nuns now raise llamas at the farm.

You don't suppose the farm being turned into a religious retreat had anything to do with Anna's miraculous birth, do you? Nah!

Rick's Cattalo Show at a Michigan county fair.

Joe and Karen back on the road operating Rick's Coyote Café at the Dodge County Fair in Beaver Dam, Wisconsin, 1994. Charbroiled butterfly pork chops, giant onion rings, cowboy cold slaw, baked beans, and coyote burgers were on the food trailer's menu.

Rick's Coyote Café ready for the road, 1994.

CHAPTER IX
Big Jim, the Giant Horse
1 1/4 Tons of Beauty!

I wanted to learn everything I could about draft horses and horse pulls (a competition between teams of horses to see who could pull the most weight). Robert Dunton showed and raised purebred Belgian draft horses for most of his life. So, when I met Robert at a Michigan fair during my 1974 summer tour, I sought his friendship and advice.

Robert's teenage son, Randy, loved sideshows, and I spent hours talking to him about the best ones I had seen. Randy's father and I became good friends, and Bob tipped me off about an opportunity to buy one of the biggest horses he had ever seen.

Big Jim the Giant Horse, an oversized Belgian gelding born to normal-sized parents in Canada. He stood over 19 hands (standard horse measurement) or 6'7" at his shoulder. He weighed 2,800 pounds—"that's 1¼ tons of brute strength!" Jim munched down 30 pounds of grain and a bale of hay per day to ease his hunger pains. "Big Jim's" owner, Rick West, says, "You have to see it to believe it... we didn't believe it ourselves until we saw it!"

Cheap thrills at the Alabama State Fair. As Rick brought his horses out for a newspaper photographer, a crowd of fairgoers quickly gathered for a free peek.

At first sight, he was huge—gargantuan! The horse measured nearly 20 hands tall (6'7") at his withers (shoulders) and weighed twenty-eight hundred pounds. The giant horse was sorrel in color, with a white mane and six-foot-long tail. The crest of its mammoth neck was far and away the biggest I had ever seen on a horse.

The horse had a presence about him. After a little negotiation, the owner and I agreed upon a price, and I now owned Big Jim, the Giant Horse.

Jim had competed in horse-pulling events and was a little jumpy at times. Fireworks, balloons breaking, and kids screaming sometimes spooked him, and if anyone happened to be exercising him at the time, Jim would run off, dragging his handler along. Big Jim reminded me of Bozo, my uncle's first giant steer, who dragged cousin Wayne and me around many county fairs.

One night at the Dickson County Fair in Tennessee, Jim got loose while we were exercising him and ran through the darkened dairy barn, jumping over cattle exhibitors who were sleeping on cots in the aisleway. Luckily, no one was hurt, but people got scared. You should have heard the near-death stories circulating around the fairgrounds the next day!

Another time, while playing Belmont County Fair in St. Clairsville, Ohio, my cousin, Allen Vanden Plas, took Jim out for a television feature to be aired on the 6 o'clock news. Their interview was held on the football field next to the fairgrounds. As it commenced, the local high school team unexpectedly charged out of the locker room and onto the field.

"Keep the camera rolling!" an excited reporter yelled to his cameraman. That evening, the newscast opened with some great footage of Big Jim tearing across the football field dragging Allen along behind.

Rick doing a segment for the 6 o'clock news in Harlingen, Texas, 1980.

Rick and his cousin Allen beside Rick's 1972 Chevy, 1977.

When traveling between shows, we would stop at truck stops every six hours to rest the animals. As we unloaded Big Jim, his size caused curious onlookers and gawkers to bombard us with never-ending questions.

The first summer I took Big Jim out, Joe and Karen's sons, Joey, 9, and Jesse, 8, helped me. The boys and I traveled to the Dane County Fair in Madison, Wisconsin, and set up outside the coliseum where Fleetwood Mac was scheduled to play.

That night we were plenty busy; unfortunately I experienced one of my debilitating migraine headaches. I went to the camper reluctantly, planning to lie down and get some sleep. Hopefully, when I awakened, the disabling ache would be gone.

As I walked away, I told the young boys, who were wary of the horse, to come get me if they had any trouble. Fortunately for me, those boys were responsible. They didn't come to get me until 1 a.m. The fair had closed, and my headache was gone.

"Rick, we made a whole lot of money," Joey said. "We hid it under the hay bale in the corner. Can you go get it? We were afraid to walk to the camper carrying it."

Those boys did themselves proud that night. It's too bad that times have changed. These days, you can't let two young boys run a show alone at a big fair.

Joey and Jesse Cisneroz with Rick and his sister, Vicki, ready to start a tour of the summer fairs with "Big Jim."

"Big Jim's" portable barn at the Tulsa State Fair.

One time I was showing Big Jim at a shopping center in a small town in Texas, when a representative of the local humane society came by and asked to speak with the owner.

"That would be me," I told her.

She looked irritated. She started complaining that Jim's food dish was empty, he didn't get any exercise, we were showing him for money, and he looked so sad.

"Well, ma'am," I explained, "if you kept grain in front of a horse all the time, he would over-eat and founder. You're not suggesting that I do that, are you?"

She stammered a bit and said, "Of course not."

"Well now, take a good look at Jim. You can see he isn't missing any meals! After all, he does weigh twenty-eight hundred pounds."

I described the care we gave Jim and how we took him out for exercise every day. I wasn't sure how much of what I had to say was getting through to her. She cut me off.

"He would be better off dead!" she cried out.

The cruel remark caught me by surprise. I turned red from anger and snapped, "Excuse me, but are you under psychiatric care, or what?"

Our conversation ended there. She left in a huff.

Another time I was playing the Canfield, Ohio, fair when four or five horse pullers began to taunt me, giving me a hard time inside my own exhibit. The pot-bellied leader of the group, wearing a dirty John Deere baseball cap and well-worn bib overalls, razzed me about his big horse, a horse that was supposedly a lot larger than Big Jim.

Rick gives "Big Jim" a workout on a two-wheeled draft-horse cart. Jim's harness had to be specially made because of his gargantuan size.

BIG DRAWS

Gargantuan animals add a surreal note to county fair

By Andrew Weiland
of The Press Staff

PLYMOUTH — He eats 8 gallons of grain and a bale of hay everyday. When he's thirsty he drinks up to 20 gallons of water a day.

What single living thing could possibly eat and drink so much in just 24 short hours? How about a 2,600-pound horse with an appetite to match?

That would be Big Jim, one of four out-sized animals on display just inside the gate at the Sheboygan County Fair. It costs 50 cents to see each of the animals.

At 19 hands high (that's a standard horse measurement — a "hand" is about four inches) the 16-year old Belgian is only two hands short of the biggest horse ever.

Rick West of Nacogdoches, Texas proudly shows off his unique animals. Besides Big Jim, there's a huge pig named Boss Hog, an unusually lengthy alligator named Ali and a miniature stallion named Wizard.

Traveling sideshows like these have faded dramatically from fairs and carnivals since their heydays in the 1960s, West said. Sideshows involving people were outlawed primarily because many felt they were demeaning.

But West has been running sideshows like this for many years and shows no sign of giving up his interesting way of making a living.

"I've done it all my life," he said. "People still like to see it, there's just not as many people doing it."

The sideshows helped West pay his way through college. Originally from Wisconsin, he moved to Texas after school to take care of his animals. He doesn't raise the big creatures, but instead gets tips from people who sell their over-sized or unusual animals.

"I've never tried to grow one myself,"

Turn to BIG DRAWS/A4

Rick West shows off Big Jim, his 2,600-pound horse, which is on display at the Sheboygan County Fair. Big Jim is one of four unique animals in a traveling sideshow run by West. Fairgoers who want to see the animals must pay 50 cents each.

Apparently, they were having a little fun at my expense while waiting for the scheduled pulling contest. The pullers told people already inside my exhibit that their pulling horse was much bigger than Big Jim. Then they stood out in front of my barn hollering, laughing, and telling people not to go in and see Big Jim because he wasn't worth the twenty-five cents admission. These guys were really getting on my nerves!

"Big Draws," a news article from the front page of The Sheboygan Press, Wisconsin, 1999.

61

Staff photo by David Woodard

BIG JIM, an oversized Belgium breed horse, nuzzles Mr. Wizard, a miniature horse, while owner Rick West holds the reins. The tournament

AN EXOTIC FAMILY
Local man travels with his unusual pets

By EMILY MORRIS
Sentinel Staff

Some people like to live large — Rick West takes it to the extreme.

West lives on Star Farm off Highway 7 West in Nacogdoches. He has a horse, a pig and an alligator that may very well be

among the largest of their kind in the world. Big Jim, Wizard and Boss Hog are West's claim to fame, and he's on the road with them about three months out of the year.

He said the animals are like family members, and that's how he treats them.

West said his fascination with exotic animals started 34 years ago.

"My uncle was a meat inspector in Wisconsin," he said. "Someone had brought a 3,000-pound Holstein steer in for slaughter. My uncle was amazed and thought people might be interested in seeing it. He bought it, and got an army tent to set up at the fair. I

Please see EXOTIC, Page 6A

"Some people like to live large—Rick West takes it to the extreme!" A front-page article from The Daily Sentinel, Nacogdoches, Texas, 1997.

One of Rick's "Big Jim" horses, called "Red" when he wasn't on tour.

After they left, I put five one-hundred-dollar bills in my pocket and headed over to the grandstand infield, where their trucks and horse trailers were parked. The first thing I did was check out the horse they had been raving about. It was nowhere near as big as Jim.

The ringleader who had given me most of the trouble was standing by his so-called giant horse. I walked up to him, held my five bills into the air and announced in a loud voice, "I have $500 that I will pay to anyone with a horse bigger than Big Jim!"

Everybody stopped talking, and the pullers and their friends stared at me. These were betting boys, no doubt about it. If they were looking for action, I'd give them some. "Now, where is that big horse you claim to have?" I asked. "We can weigh the horses right here on the fairground scales."

"Errr-ah," he mumbled.

"C'mon, let's put some real money up," I said loudly.

"Alright, calm down," he said.

"Yeah, take it easy kid," one of the other pullers yelled.

"Hey," I said, staring my tormenter squarely in the eye, "if you don't have five hundred dollars, maybe some of your buddies could chip in to win some of this easy money. It's time to put up, or shut up!"

Four of Rick's shows at the Mecosta County Fair in Big Rapids, Michigan.

Rick's friend, Tom Smith, and Big Jim the Giant Horse.

"Hey kid, we were just joking, okay?" I heard someone behind me say.

They didn't want to bet. They didn't want to brag any more. Instead, they were pleading with me to go away.

Well, I didn't find their shenanigans funny, but I did get a chance to make my point. Big Jim was the *star* of this fair.

Before long, I had framed out three "Big Jim Shows," and was showing these great horses at state and county fairs all over America.

See Big Jim, the Giant Horse. A horse that stands nearly 20 hands tall at his withers, or 6'7" at his shoulders. A horse that weighs 2,800 lbs. That's over 1¼ tons of beauty! Feet the size of nail kegs! He's alive. He's real. The biggest horse you will ever see! 1¼ tons of brute strength! You have to see it to believe it; we didn't believe it ourselves until we saw it. See Big Jim, the Giant Horse.

CHAPTER X
Holy Cow!
Ten Thousand Hamburgers on the Hoof!

In November 1974 I received an interesting phone call. "Hello, my name is John McKinney," a male voice with a New England accent said. "I live in upstate New York. I've been hearing about your animal exhibits and thought since you're in the business, you might be interested in the big steer I have. He weighs 3,500 pounds, and I think he could make you a ton of money."

"Where did you get the steer?" I asked.

"My teenage daughter," he answered. "She got him as a calf, for her 4-H project. She's been raising him, but he's gotten too big. We raise horses and just don't have room for the big steer."

Not a lot of people are interested in buying such a big animal, because caring for it requires a lot of work and a mountain of feed. John and I talked price, and I thought the amount he asked was too high. Nevertheless, I told him I would like to take a look at his steer.

In January 1975, my brother-in-law, Joe, and I headed toward John's upstate New York farm in my Datsun pickup.

"Rural Greenleaf Couple Really Big in Livestock," article featuring Big Bill the Giant Steer and Rick's other unusual animals, 1978.

After meeting John, we headed out to the barn. Just like he said, the steer was a giant. The animal possessed an amazing bulk from the top of his back down to the bottom of his stomach. He also had a nice matching pair of upswept horns. The steer was a good-looking animal, and I really liked him.

However, I felt the giant steer was worth only a third of John's asking price. During lunch I made John a respectable counteroffer that he didn't even consider. That was it as far as he was concerned; we were done talking.

In the morning Joe and I headed home—without the steer. As we drove westward on the New York State Thruway we ran headlong into a major winter blizzard barreling toward the East Coast. It snowed so hard I couldn't see the painted centerline on the Interstate. I felt like someone threw a white blanket over my windshield. Snow actually came down in clumps, and built up on the windshield wipers.

I had to stop occasionally to bang snow off the wiper blades so they would work. To see where I was driving, I used the mile markers along the shoulder of the road that stuck up out of the snow.

Eventually, we no longer saw any vehicles on the highway. The only cars and trucks we did see were in the ditch. We arrived at a truck stop and strolled inside for lunch.

"How did you guys get here?" a truck driver asked.

"In my Datsun pickup," I answered.

"Aw, come on, I'm not believing that one!" he replied.

I couldn't believe the reception we received. Apparently, we were the only people still on the Interstate. The truckers peered outside looking for a four-wheel-drive pickup with chains. Once they saw the Datsun and began to believe me, the big-rig drivers implored us to stay until the storm let up.

"You can't go back out there," one guy argued. "Even the snowplows have stopped running."

"Hey, we're from Wisconsin," I joked. "We're not afraid of a little snow."

Well, we managed to drive until we reached barricades that the State Highway Patrol had erected at Buffalo, directing us to a turnpike exit ramp and an overnight stay at a motel. Watching the evening news, we learned the governor had declared a State of Emergency and shut down the Thruway due to the ferocity of the storm! (The blizzard dumped twenty-four inches of wet snow in 36 hours, burying roadways and tying up traffic from Chicago to New York City.)

I knew there wasn't a big market, other than my uncle, for giant steers. Sure enough, after a couple months passed, John called to find out if my counteroffer was still on the table. I said yes, and I made arrangements to drive back to New York and pick up the steer. On the return trip, I took my '72 Chevy pickup and a twenty-foot livestock trailer.

Once I got back to John's farm, I noticed the steer had torn off the gates and sides of three horse stalls. I wondered, "Did I make a mistake? Would he be too hard to handle?"

Rick's niece, Anna Cisneroz, learning to lead "Big Bill."

After all, he was huge and very agile. Well, I figured our first test would be loading him into the trailer. I tried to calculate the easiest way to get him loaded.

Joe and I led the giant steer to the entrance, and guess what? He went right in. Hey, this was easy! We named him Bill and headed back to Wisconsin.

Everything was going great until we stopped that night. Joe and I were tired, and we needed to catch a few hours sleep. We unloaded Bill and tied him to the back of the trailer. Once Bill's view of us was blocked, he started bellowing, "Moooo-ahhhh!"

The silence barely covered up the sound before the plaintive voice pierced the night again, this time louder. "Moooo-ahhhh!" The bellowing complaint grew louder and louder until the truck's windows rattled.

"He's big alright," I thought, "and that includes his voice!" I lay in the truck with eyes wide open for a good half-hour until I heard Bill's voice grow hoarse. I opened the cab's door, and walked over to the steer. Bill looked at me in relief and settled down.

Bill was afraid to be alone! This great big steer was, in reality, very gentle. Joe had to babysit Bill all night or he wouldn't keep quiet. I had to get some sleep; Joe could sleep in the truck tomorrow while I drove.

This wasn't the only time Bill showed his fear of being left alone. When we tore down and loaded his portable barn at the end of the fair, he would bellow until we loaded him too. I guess he didn't want us to forget and leave him at the fairgrounds!

"Big Bill," his stage name, was the biggest baby I ever saw. When I took people out to see him, as soon as we walked within eyesight, he ran toward me as fast as he could. Everyone around me scattered. They didn't know Bill was just happy to see me and would stop when he got close. I just hoped he wouldn't trip as he put on the brakes!

Holy Cow! Rick and his 3,500-pound giant steer "Big Bill," on the front page of the Kokomo Tribune, 1982.

"Big Bill the Giant Steer," one of several portable displays Rick framed out to show his unusual animals. The display broke down to twelve pieces plus three roof braces. Rick and a helper set it up and were ready to open within an hour. His sister, Vicki, manned the ticket box.

When Bill felt it was time to go back to the show after his nightly exercise, he'd just head back, stand by the barn door and wait for me if I wasn't there. Most touching of all, Bill loved to be rubbed along his dewlap (the loose part of a cow's skin, which helps cool the animal, extending from the throat down along the chest). As I rubbed him, he would raise his head and close his eyes. Then his eyes would start to moisten. And if I continued to rub him softly, tears flowed down his cheeks.

One time when I was playing a Deridder, Louisiana, shopping center, I put a lead rope on each side of Bill's halter to use as reins, rode him bareback over to the Dairy Queen® drive-through and ordered a milkshake through the intercom. The kids working that night were pretty surprised when I rode up to the pickup window to pay!

I exhibited Big Bill at the Sumter County Fair in Americus, Georgia (President Jimmy Carter's hometown fair), when his notorious brother Billy presented himself with a great deal of self-importance. (Remember Billy Beer?) Well this squat, rotund fellow never introduced himself, but tried to walk right in and see my giant steer without paying.

Well, everyone there may have known Billy, but we didn't! Dean Vanden Heuvel, who was manning my ticket box at the time, grabbed Billy by the arm to explain that the admission price to see this exhibit was twenty-five cents. Before Billy could respond, two Secret Service agents suddenly appeared in dark business suits and black spit-shined shoes. "We have it," one of them yelled, as his partner scrambled to dig some quarters out of his pockets.

Big Bill loved cotton candy and was always begging to get some from the kids. If a youngster didn't secure his cotton candy properly, Bill would stretch his head out through the bars of his pen and wrap his long tongue around the sweet, pink fluff. You couldn't help thinking Bill was cute, unless you were the kid whose cotton candy had just been stolen.

HOLY COW... IT'S BIG BILL THE GIANT STEER

BIG BILL is a Holstein Steer, born of normal parents on a dairy farm in Upper New York State. He weighs approximately 3,500 pounds, stands 6 feet at the shoulder and can raise his head to a height well over 7 feet. It is estimated that Big Bill would make over 10,000 hamburgers...that's over 1½ tons of beef on the hoof! "But don't worry, says Rick West, Bill's owner; we don't ever intend to butcher him...he's part of the family". Big Bill is fed 40 pounds of specially mixed grains a day plus a bale of hay. When Big Bill is not on tour, he spends the rest of the year at Star Farm, Nacogdoches, Texas.

"Holy Cow!" story for a shopping center date.

BIG THINGS HAPPENIN' AT THE PLAZA!

"BIG JIM" 2600 lbs. (ADMISSION) "BIG BILL" 3500 lbs

See Them Now Thru SATURDAY MAY 17th

HILLTOP PLAZA SHOPPING CENTER
OVER 3 TONS OF BEAUTY ON DISPLAY!

Newspaper ad for a shopping center "still date," 1979.

Rick and his oversized bovine at Star Farm North, Greenleaf, Wisconsin.

Rick's brother-in-law, Joe Cisneroz, sizing up Jack Mericle's steer, Satan, at the Texas State Fair in Dallas.

Rick and Bozo the Giant Steer splashed across the front page of the Daily News, Bowling Green, Kentucky, July 7, 1969.

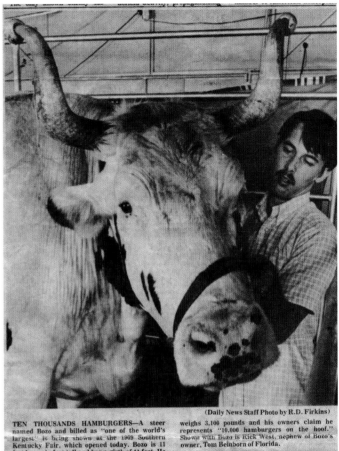

(Daily News Staff Photo by R.D. Firkins)

TEN THOUSANDS HAMBURGERS—A steer named Bozo and billed as "one of the world's largest" is being shown at the 1969 Southern Kentucky Fair, which opened today. Bozo is 11 feet long, six feet tall and has a girth of 11 feet. He weighs 3,100 pounds and his owners claim he represents "10,000 hamburgers on the hoof." Shown with Bozo is Rick West, nephew of Bozo's owner, Tom Beinborn of Florida.

Rick and Bozo the Giant Steer at the Ohio State Fair, 1968.

Long after his demise, I still maintain a soft spot in my heart for that steer. He was more than an exhibit...he was Big Bill.

Holy cow! It's Big Bill, the Giant Steer. A giant in the cattle industry... a steer two to three times normal size. See a steer that's eleven feet around and eleven feet long. A steer that stands six feet tall at his shoulders. A steer that can raise his head to a height well over seven feet... 10,000 hamburgers on the hoof!... This is no bum steer folks, he's real, he's alive, you know he's alive, you can smell him. A steer that weighs over 3,500 pounds... That's over 1 1/2 tons of brute strength! You'll never see so-o-o much for so little. See Big Bill, the Giant Steer.

Rick with one of his uncle's giant steers, Mikey, who was six feet tall and weighed 3,300 pounds. Mikey was an Italian Chianina, the largest breed of cattle in the world.

Barron Lyndall, billed as the "Largest Steer in the World," while "Woodmen of the World" lined up in front of the Texas bally platform, 1905. The ticket-taker, dressed in her Sunday best, worked the ticket box while the talker in his top hat and suit drew attention to the big banner advertising the mammoth bovine.

1945 Animal Oddities poster featuring a 3,005-pound bovine labeled, "The World's Largest Steer."

CHAPTER XI
Hog Heaven
1,100 lbs. of Bacon Bits on the Hoof!

While playing the Tulsa State Fair during the 1980s, a hog farmer from Coweta, Oklahoma, came up to one of my shows looking to sell his huge, red Duroc boar (male hog). I enjoyed great success showing mammoth animals that turned out to be lovable giants, and his well-proportioned 1,100-pound hog appeared to be no exception. In fact, the giant porker acted more like a big puppy than an overgrown hog. So I bought him and named him Harley.

I was surprised how much people love hogs... the bigger the better. And Harley really seemed to love all the attention. It seemed natural to call him "Boss Hog" when we displayed him at the fairs.

Whenever it was suppertime at the farm, Harley came running and jumping with so much enthusiasm that all four feet left the ground. Watching Harley race to his feeding trough was quite a sight. That hog didn't miss any meals!

My neighbor, Chris, discovered the hog loved donuts—not just any donuts, mind you, but chocolate donuts. On frequent visits to my farm, Chris would bring along a dozen donuts and ride the big hog around bareback after Harley finished making a pig out of himself.

Front-page story from The Daily Sentinel, Nacogdoches, Texas, 1997. Before the Green Bay Packers played the New England Patriots in the 1997 Super Bowl, my brother-in-law sent two of the Packer fans' notorious Cheeseheads® hats for Chris (Harley's chocolate doughnut supplier) and me to wear during the game. My mom also shipped some chili from Green Bay's famous Chili John's restaurant. Packers won 35-21.

PACKER BACKERS

Staff photo by Dave Rossman

RICK WEST, left, and Chris Englert sport cheese hats a friend sent from Wisconsin.

Die-hard Green Bay fans will be wearing cheese, eating chili

Fairgoers line up to gawk at Rick West's "Biggest Pig." The Giant Hog weighed in at over 1,100 pounds.
That's over half a ton of pork on the hoof. "Look at the size of the pork chops on this one!"

Rick and his prodigious porker at the farm.

Harley possessed another endearing trait. If he saw me working down by the barn, he started grunting. He continued the noise until I gave him some attention or a vigorous scratch behind the ears.

Boss Hog knew the sound of my voice without ever seeing me, too. Whenever he heard my voice at the fair, he began a grunting routine. I'd reply by asking him how he was doing, and he would continue the conversation, "Grunt, grunt, grunt."

As long as I talked to him, he grunted back, just like we were having a real back-and-forth dialogue. Whenever I ignored him and he needed to get my attention, his grunts became more urgent. But during our many conversations, he spoke softer.

Like any well-nurtured hog, Harley's favorite activities were eating and sleeping. He usually slept for two to three hours at a time, much to the disappointment of the people viewing him.

Rick West of Nacogdoches, Texas, washes down the roof of his 'Biggest Pig' exhibit at the State Fairgrounds. West also has an alligator and a miniature horse in his stable for viewing. The Alabama State Fair will open tomorrow.
Stephen Gates/Post-Herald

Rick washing the Biggest Pig display in preparation for the Alabama State Fair's opening, 1991.

I put in a lot of twelve to fourteen hour days in the ticket box answering the same old questions hour after hour:

"How much does he eat?"

"Does he sleep all the time?"

"Does he ever get up?"

"Is he too big to get up?"

And the most commonly asked question: "Can you make him get up?"

Some people realized we were open all day and knew my hog needed to rest, too. But other people poked, or even slapped, him, figuring they could wake up Harley by disturbing him.

One particularly obnoxious customer slapped Harley in front of me, and I almost lost my cool. "What did you do that for?" I snapped.

"Hey, I paid to see him standing up," the mooch complained.

"It's only 50 cents," I said contemptuously. "You're paying for a look at him, so here he is. He may be sleeping, he may be eating, he may be awake, he may be standing up, but he doesn't do any tricks.

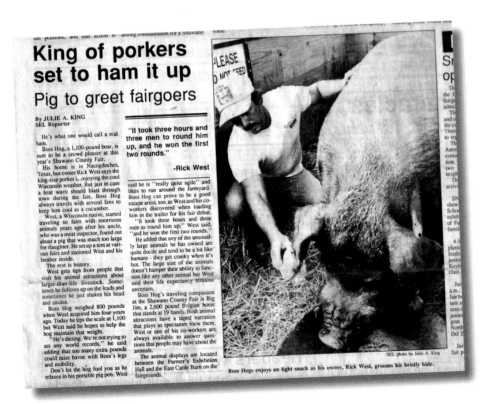

King of porkers set to ham it up
Pig to greet fairgoers

By JULIE A. KING
SEL Reporter

He's what one would call a real ham. Boss Hog, a 1,100-pound boar, is sure to be a crowd pleaser at this year's Shawano County Fair.

His home is in Nacogdoches, Texas, but owner Rick West says the king-size porker is enjoying the cool Wisconsin weather. But just in case a heat wave should blast through town during the fair, Boss Hog always travels with several fans to keep him cool as a cucumber.

West, a Wisconsin native, started traveling to fairs with enormous animals years ago after his uncle, who was a meat inspector, found out about a pig that was much too large for slaughter. He set up a tent at various fairs and stationed West and his brother inside.

The rest is history.

West gets tips from people that visit his animal attractions about larger-than-life livestock. Sometimes he follows up on the leads and sometimes he just shakes his head and smiles.

Boss Hog weighed 800 pounds when West acquired him four years ago. Today he tips the scale at 1,100 but West said he hopes to help the hog maintain that weight.

"He's dieting. We're not trying to set any world records," he said adding that too many extra pounds could raise havoc with Boss's legs and mobility.

Don't let the hog fool you as he relaxes in his portable pig pen. West

"It took three hours and three men to round him up, and he won the first two rounds."

-Rick West

said he is "really quite agile" and likes to run around the farmyard. Boss Hog can prove to be a good escape artist, too, as West and his co-workers discovered when loading him in the trailer for his fair debut.

"It took three hours and three men to round him up," West said, "and he won the first two rounds."

He added that any of the unusually large animals he has owned are quite docile and tend to be a bit like humans - they get cranky when it's hot. The large size of the animals doesn't hamper their ability to function like any other animal but West said their life expectancy remains uncertain.

Boss Hog's traveling companion at the Shawano County Fair is Big Jim, a 2,600 pound Belgian horse that stands at 19 hands. Both animal attractions have a taped narration that plays as spectators view them. West or one of his co-workers are always available to answer questions that people may have about the animals.

The animal displays are located between the Farmer's Exhibition Hall and the East Cattle Barn on the fairgrounds.

Boss Hogs enjoys an light snack as his owner, Rick West, grooms his bristly hide.
SEL photo by Julie A. King

"King of the Porkers," hamming it up at the Shawano County Fair, 1988.

"The sign says, 'Do Not Touch.' That's what it means; this is not a petting zoo. You're here only to view the animal. Now, be nice to Boss or I'm going to toss you off the show!"

When you spend time with an animal, day in and day out over the years, you get pretty attached. If someone slaps your animal, you get the same feeling as if you were slapped. In fact, I'd rather be the one who was slapped.

It's human nature. A hundred people can tell you how much they love your exhibit, but if one mooch gives you a hard time, that's the guy you remember when you go to bed that night.

A few years back, a representative of David Letterman's show contacted me about bringing Boss Hog to the "Big Apple." David was planning a bit about county fairs, and the show's producer was given my name. Unfortunately, by the time he got in touch with me, only two days were left before the show was to be taped.

New York is a long drive from east Texas. Plus there were a few details to work out, like where do you park a truck and thirty-two-foot livestock trailer on Fifth Avenue? Not to mention how to maneuver the hog up an elevator, and finding rubber mats to cover the studio's slick, polished floor.

My sideshow life is just like television; it's part of show business. I'm the one who knows how to transport giant animals, and I could see there wasn't enough time to make the show on such short notice.

Biggest Pig Show at the Warren County Agricultural Fair, Lebanon, Ohio, sporting the original roof sign, 1989.

78

It was too bad. Boss Hog's national television debut would have been a hoot. He would have garnered a lot of TV exposure, especially if he had gotten loose into the audience or peed on the floor!

Holy hog, it's Boss Hog, the giant pig! A pig two to three times normal size. A pig that stands four feet tall. A pig that's ten feet long. A pig that weighs over 1,100 lbs... that's right, over half-a-ton of pork on the hoof. Look at the size of the pork chops on this one! See Boss Hog, the giant pig. And he's alive, he's real... 1,100 lbs. of bacon bits on the hoof! Holy hog, look at the size of pork chops on this one!

Boss Hog taking a little afternoon siesta, his favorite pastime!

Chapter XII
New York Alligators
Unchanged since the Dinosaur Age!

Ever hear about the alligators in the sewers of New York? Sure, you have.

As the legend goes, some young boys received the tiny critters as gifts from their parents' winter trips to Florida. The boys eventually grew tired of what were really baby alligators, and flushed them down the toilet into the sewer where they grew to monstrous size. Well, this story isn't about one of those gators.

In May 1988 a schoolteacher in Mechanicville, New York called. He had bought a large Florida alligator and was exhibiting it at fairs in New York State. His exhibit wasn't making money because he didn't know much about the sideshow business. He asked me if I wanted to buy the gator and display trailer.

I made him an offer and four months later—after Labor Day—he agreed to my price. This was the second time a New Yorker asked if I wanted to buy his monstrous animal; the giant steer was the first. What made this coincidence even more eerie is that both sellers asked for the same amount of money. And after negotiation, I wound up paying the identical amount for each one too!

Anyway, I have digressed from my story. A couple weeks after our verbal agreement, I drove to Mechanicville in my '72 Chevy pickup. As I looked the exhibit over, I saw the schoolteacher had bought a nice gator but didn't know the first thing about framing a grind show.

Tom Smith helping Rick check the shows.

The Giant Alligator Show that Rick framed, 1989.

The front confused folks; people had no idea what was inside. Unwittingly, he had violated the cardinal rule of sideshow display: If people have to ask what's in your exhibit, you're not making any money.

I hitched up the "fearsome, man-eating alligator" trailer, and drove back to the fair in lower Michigan where my shows were set up, arriving in time to show the twelve-foot reptile during the fair's final weekend. I had a new sign painted so fairgoers at least knew what I had on exhibit. The gator took in enough paid admissions during that weekend to recoup my entire investment. I exhibited the gator at my few remaining fairs that season and framed a new, money-making show for the alligator during the winter.

I moved around the country showing the gator along with my other exhibits, eventually playing the Alabama State Fair in Birmingham, where I was perplexed by one customer's question.

"Do he moo?" the man asked.

I know gators don't moo, and this didn't look like a cow. "Excuse me?" I said.

He asked again, "Do he moo. Do he moo?"

"Hold on a moment," I answered. I called over Claude, an Alabama friend better known to fairgoers as the "Gatorman," to see if he could decipher the man's question.

Claude asked the man to repeat his question and then chuckled. "He just wants to know if the alligator ever moved," he explained.

Well, we all enjoyed a good laugh, the customer included. But to this day, we acknowledge my difficulty in understanding Alabamese by asking one another, "Do he moo?"

Claude has helped me with the Gator Show for over eighteen years. His "Gatorman" accent is as thick as the humid Alabama air on a muggy August evening. And Claude's sun-worn skin looks as rough as the hide on my big old alligator.

Rick's mom helping out at the Giant Alligator Show.

It's done with mirrors! Rick walking a baby gator in front of the Giant Alligator Show before the fair began.

Rick with a baby gator working the front of the Giant Alligator Show at the Ionia, Michigan, Free Fair, 1990.

You might be interested to know the New York Alligator wasn't my first reptile exhibit. In 1975 I imported four 6-foot water monitors from a reptile dealer in Thailand. When I went down to the airport in Chicago to pick the lizards up, customs agents insisted on opening the crate to inspect it.

These guys had no clue of the natural defense mechanisms with which the monitor lizards were equipped. Monitors are armed with razor-sharp teeth, long claws and a whip-like tail that can inflict painful welts.

I told one of the customs guys, "I don't think that is a good idea. These lizards are not that easy to handle."

He glared at me suspiciously. "You wouldn't have any contraband in there, would you? We are going to check this crate, by God. And you stay right where you are!"

His partner started prying the top open with a crowbar, causing the wooden crate's nails to groan. In response, one of the monitors inside hissed and slammed his tail against the side. That's when all hell broke loose inside the crate.

The customs officer jumped back in alarm, hammered the nails back into place, and told me they wouldn't have to open the crate after all. "Get these monsters out of here!" he yelled.

Rick and one of his imported monitor lizards.

While we framed the exhibit, brother-in-law Joe kept the monsters, I mean monitors, in his basement. The second day after I cleared customs, Joe called. "The lizards are out!" he yelled into the phone.

I didn't quite comprehend what he meant. "Out, what do you mean, they're out?" I asked.

"Well, they aren't in the cage," Joe said.

"How'd they get out?" I asked. My heart was in my throat.

"I don't know how they got out," he replied, "or where they are! Get over here—now!"

We looked around and discovered monitor lizards are amazingly strong. Even though we piled cement blocks on top of the cage, the reptiles had pried it off. We were both afraid of the lizards, but we put on leather welding gloves and used a three-foot capture pole with a noose to tighten around their necks. Eventually we rounded up all four lizards, even though each was a handful. Only one of the lizards, Rasputin, ever warmed up to being handled.

Monitor lizards love to eat eggs and baby chicks. Each lizard consumed between six to ten chicks for its weekly meal. One sound that haunted me: The last chick the lizard devoured was still chirping while the cold-blooded monitor began dining on its next victim.

Unchanged since the dinosaur age... It is like going to the zoo one hundred and thirty million years ago.

The Giant Lizard Show at the Henry County Fair in Napoleon, Ohio, 1975.

Rick gets a good grip on one of his reptilian monsters.

One of the original Giant Lizard Show panels stored in Rick's barn.

Close-up of the Giant Lizard sign, detailing the artistic prowess of Dale Kuipers.

Chapter XIII
Monkey Business
May all your days be Monkey Days!

The implausible image struck me: a black-and-white Capuchin monkey dressed up in clown costume, sitting in a red Radio Flyer® wagon. The monkey didn't do a darned thing—it just sat there on its miniature monkey chair—and the people around me threw coins into the wagon.

I couldn't believe it. That petulant monkey couldn't follow a command. It wouldn't even pay attention to his handler! The primate just sat there trying to remove its clothes.

That's how I met Norris Welch and his girlfriend, Debbie. They had recently bought their first monkey to pursue Norris' lifelong dream of becoming a successful organ grinder. He dreamed about independence—the kind that only he, Debbie, and the monkey could have—by being able to make a living on any street corner, anywhere.

Norris working the Strawberry Festival in Poteet, Texas.

Norris and Debbie had recently retired from running a "Cover-the-Spot" game, sometimes known as "The Circle of Science." Norris had become an expert thimblerigger, whose bushy, sculpted 'round-the-lips moustache accentuated his talents.

Norris told me he never gave away one prize the whole time Debbie and he ran the spot game. But he was so good at what he did that he never got any beefs, either. He gave me a board and some disks, and showed me how the brilliantly simple game works.

The agent takes a white board with an 7 1/8-inch red circular spot on it, sets the board down in front of a "mark" and hands him five, 4 3/8-inch metal discs, usually zinc. He explains to the mark that he must cover up the red on the board by dropping the five metal discs on parts of the red circle. "All you have to do is cover the spot with the five discs and you win! Here, let me show you how easily it's done." (The agent doesn't stress that if there's any red showing—even a tiny amount—the mark loses.)

Five discs can cover the spot, but remember it's a game of skill. And the agent has spent many hours honing his skills. One consolation: It's fun to try even if you don't win.

Anyway, let's get back to Norris and Debbie's new vocation. They kept trying—with limited success—to train their monkey, until they were advised to see a special woman in Florida, Rachael Lopez. Norris' burning ambition to become an organ grinder put them on a trip down South.

Mrs. Lopez turned out to be the real deal, a first-class monkey trainer who trains monkeys to work on a line (a nylon string about 15 feet long, with the excess wrapped in the handler's hand), take a coin from the fun-seeker's hand and tip his hat. Mrs. Lopez took a liking to Debbie and eventually gave training instructions over the phone, not the best way to learn the correct training techniques. However, after many phone calls Debbie had the monkey started.

A couple years later I ran into Norris and Debbie while playing the Howard County 4-H Fair in Greentown, Indiana. They billed themselves as "Fun Times and Monkey Business." Norris wore his familiar black pants and suspenders with a white shirt, bowtie, black fedora, wingtip shoes, and a gold chain on his pocket watch. He really looked the part of an Old World organ grinder. His New England accent added to the class act.

Norris, the Monkey Man.

Norris and Vinnie entertaining fairgoers at the Shawano County Fair, Shawano, Wisconsin.

To complete their monkey act, Norris and Debbie bought an ornate, red-and-gold hurdy-gurdy music box with a crank on its side. They owned four monkeys, and three of them had many years of training. The more-experienced monkeys were so well trained that they could be taken out and worked together.

One day Norris let me work Louie, the easiest-going and first monkey Debbie trained. When I grabbed hold of the leash, Louie sized me up quickly. He realized I didn't know a darned thing about working a monkey. There was no doubt in Louie's mind... I was a mark.

He soon found out just how dumb I was. Louie made me think he was headed in one direction, but he quickly moved in the other. As his reward, Louie grabbed a kid's hotdog. The monkey had played me! Fortunately, Louie decided that my monkey-handling debut would not be too disastrous.

Norris is a pretty colorful character with a lot of one-liners in his repertoire. Some of my favorites:

People will ask him why the monkey is on such a short leash. Norris replies, "I'm afraid someone would cut a long leash when I'm not looking and steal the monkey."

Other folks will ask Norris how long the monkey has to stand up. Norris will tell them, "The monkey is in training for the Marines, and will not only have to stand up straight but will have to learn to salute, too."

People ask how he trains the monkeys. He tells them, "It's the same as training children; I use a psychiatrist and Ritalin®."

Norris owns an older-model travel trailer, but don't laugh; it's paid for. He once told me, "Ricky, see all those big, new fifth-wheel campers and trucks everyone bought? Well, there are two kinds of notes: bank notes and yard notes ($100 bills). All those guys have bank notes, but the monkey man has a pocketful of yard notes."

The next story about Norris is my favorite:

A La Crosse, Wisconsin, newspaper decided to run a story about Norris and how much money he makes. Perhaps its editor dropped a few bills at the previous year's fair.

Anyway, in this business for some reason, people think they have a right to ask you how much money you make. You would never walk up to a doctor and say, "Hey, how much money do you make a year?" It's bad etiquette, right?

Well, the newspaper assigned a female reporter to interview Norris.

(The editor must have known that if the reporter were male, Norris wouldn't have given him the time of day.) She popped various forms of the offensive question several times during her interview, including asking Norris how much money the monkey took in during one day.

Norris' tolerance level went beyond the edge, and he told her straight-faced that in one year he made more money than a brain surgeon. Sure enough, when the paper came out with the reporter's story, the following headline gave Norris' remark instant credibility as it proclaimed in big type: "Monkey Man makes more than brain surgeon."

Vinnie, one of Norris's trained monkeys, checking the midway for his next mark.

Here's another Norris story:

Once when he tried to book his monkeys into the Louisiana State Fair, the fair manager, Sam Giordano, became "unavailable for calls" every time Norris phoned. So, early the next morning, Norris called as usual, asking to speak with Sam. After being told again that Sam was not available, his secretary asked, "Whom may I say called?"

Norris replied, "I'm with the internal affairs office for the State of Louisiana."

"Just a minute, please," she stammered.

Within seconds, Sam was on the phone. And Norris told him, "O-o-oh, so you can answer the phone. I played a little trick on you, Sam! It's the Monkey Man."

Needless to say, Sam didn't find the little trick funny and Norris didn't get the fair. But Norris always has a good story. Whether it comes to jackpotting with friends or separating a mark from his money, man, oh man, this guy has talent!

One thing about monkeys: They are like having a two-year-old that never grows up. They take a great deal of time and care, and you have to keep an eye on them all the time. Monkeys don't care for spectators much, because people are usually annoying them. If monkeys ever get loose, there is hell to pay.

Johnny Rivers, well known for his diving mules, had a chimpanzee get loose at the Northern Wisconsin State Fair in Chippewa Falls. The ape decided it would be fun to run amok through the competitive fruit and vegetable display. He took a bite out of a piece of prize-winning fruit, threw it in the air, and grabbed more blue ribbon pieces while scampering down the middle of the display table, fruit just a-flying.

Johnny and I were over at one of my shows when we heard the fair's public address system blare, "Johnny Rivers, please come and get your chimp out of the produce barn. Johnny, please come get your chimp. Please."

Before the chimp could be caught, he made quite a mess. Yes, indeed.

I want to tell you about another friend, Gerry Eppel. Like Norris, he had fallen in love with the organ-grinder concept. So, when he met Norris at a San Antonio flea market, one thing led to another. Norris told him where to buy an imported monkey, whom he named "Minnie the Mooch," and Debbie helped train her.

Minnie has real quick hands and can take in a lot of coins in a ridiculously brief period of time. But once she gets them in her apron, she gets a little protective of the coins and doesn't like to let Gerry get them out.

Organ grinder Gerry Eppel with his panhandling star, Minnie the Mooch.

Another popular attraction on the midway was the Monkey Speedway, where daredevil monkeys raced around an oval track in miniature cars. Harry and Beatrice Fee operated the last big monkey speedway to tour the fairs. In 2007, Rick acquired one of the couple's original monkey cars and lighted racetrack sign. The sign, suspended over the track, was wired so the name of the winning monkey would light up at the end of each race.

"Oh Minnie," he would ask, "what are you going to do with all those coins?"

You might not expect an organ grinder to be into the latest computer and wireless technologies, but Gerry loves all the new gadgets. He always uses the latest-model cell phone, owns a laptop computer, and sports a handheld Palm Pilot® connecting him wirelessly to the Internet. He connects to the Internet at home with an ultra-high speed satellite connection, which I'm sure he'll be rigging up to use at the fairs.

Gerry doesn't work his monkey under extreme weather conditions because changes in climate can make a monkey sick. Organ grinders—at least, the smart ones—only work their monkeys on mild, warm sunny days. I coined an expression for such a great fair day... "Monkey Day."

On the other hand, if a fair day turns out to be cold, rainy or scorching hot, you might hear someone say, "This sure ain't no 'Monkey Day'."

Anyway, as I said earlier, Norris told Gerry Eppel where he could obtain a monkey. He gave Gerry the name of Todd Tucker, a 20-year-old man in central Texas who imported monkeys to sell and also owned two organ-grinding monkeys named Filo and Andrew. Todd subsequently sold Gerry his first monkey.

Todd was murdered, not long after Gerry bought his monkey, by a guy Todd had hired to drive his motorhome from venue to venue. On the trip back after playing some California spots in 1991, the perpetrator shot Todd in the head with his own gun, intending to steal the monkeys and motor home. The killer was caught at the border checkpoint west of Las Cruces, New Mexico, before he could ditch the bloody body. The impact of Todd's murder and plight of his orphaned monkeys was widely felt. The story was written up in the *National Enquirer*, and my friend, Norris, served as a pallbearer at Todd's funeral, definitely not a Monkey Day.

The bottom of the monkey car's chassis. Automotive windshield wiper arms glided over metal rails supplying 110 volts of power to the drill.

A $10 electric drill was used as a motor on the monkey cars. Using a bicycle chain, a sprocket on the drill connected to another sprocket on one rear wheel. The design proved to be inexpensive and quite durable. Following a little cleaning and tinkering, Rick returned the car to running condition.

CHAPTER XIV
Shocked and Amazed
Strange, Bizarre, the Unusual!

People have always been attracted to the strange, the bizarre, the wondrous, and the unusual. Human anomalies and freak animals fascinate us. We are not only attracted to the strange and unexplained, we are willing to pay to gawk at it.

During the Middle Ages, royalty presented human oddities like dwarfs and giants to entertain the court. P. T. Barnum's American Museum, located at Broadway and Ann Street in lower Manhattan until 1865, was world famous. Under one roof, he displayed the Feejee Mermaid, Tom Thumb, Shakespearean plays, a working reproduction of Niagara Falls, and live whales in the basement. Barnum had his finger on the pulse of what people wanted to see, understood mass advertising and put together "The Greatest Show on Earth."

In 1885, a speeding train derailed after striking Jumbo the Elephant, killing Barnum's beloved floppy-eared giant. Barnum not only had Jumbo stuffed; he had the skeleton mounted too! Barnum turned Jumbo's demise into two spectacular displays.

Nowadays, smart phones, 3D TVs, touch-screen tablets, and bottled water are in vogue, and the display of freaks in exhibits on carnival midways is considered tasteless and politically incorrect. Yet our attraction to the strange, the bizarre, and the unusual have not changed. So where do we get our fix?

The Rolling Stones, Marilyn Manson, and World Wrestling Entertainment® all use colorful sideshow elements to showcase their performances. Shock magic acts like Penn and Teller or the Jim Rose Circus Sideshow play theaters and colleges. Let's not forget films, which had their start in the dime museum, or the Smithsonian Museums' large collection of strange and unusual artifacts. There's no problem with it being considered politically incorrect; it's educational, after all. And did I mention the peep show in your home, better known as TV?

That's where you can stare at tattooed and pierced people on the Learning Channel, watch a story about Percilla the Monkey Girl on the Discovery Channel, or gawk at strange African rites of passage customs on Nat Geo TV, all wrapped up in an aura of respectability.

And don't forget regularly scheduled TV sideshows like Tyra Banks, Maury Povitch, and last, but certainly not least, Jerry Springer! We still want to look—we have to look—but we have an overwhelming need to wrap it up in such a way that it doesn't transgress our so-called "modern sensibilities."

A few traditional sideshows are still touring fairs around the country. If you get a chance to see one, don't miss it, because they are disappearing fast. It just may be the last time you get to peek at this colorful midway tradition before it's only a glorious memory.

Times have changed, and the high cost of presenting top-quality exhibits, like the big ten-in-one sideshows and girl reviews, was the major factor for their decline. All the new stuff is okay, I guess. But I sure miss those old, traditional carnival sideshows with their colorful bannerlines, spellbinding talkers, and captivating ballys.

I sure would like to go back to their heyday and see it all one more time.

GEN. TOM THUMB, WIFE & CHILD.

Barnum purchased Jumbo, the World's Largest Elephant, for $10,000 in 1882 from the Royal Zoological Society in London. Unfortunately, on September 15, 1885 in Ontario, Canada, Jumbo was struck by a freight train and killed. As news of the accident made the front page of newspapers worldwide, Barnum had Jumbo stuffed and continued showing the giant pachyderm, demonstrating he was not one to lose sleep over spilt milk.

Charles A. Stratton and his wife, Lavinia, better known as Mr. and Mrs. Tom Thumb. When Tom started work at P. T. Barnum's American Museum in 1842, his salary was only three dollars a week. But through Barnum's advertising genius, Tom Thumb became the most famous miniature person in the world. Tom toured the world, making appearances before Queen Victoria of England, Isabella of Spain, King Leopold of Brussels, King Louis Philippe of France, and U.S. President Abraham Lincoln.

NELLIE KEELER,
11 years of age, 28 inches high, weight 12lbs.
To be seen only in the Great P. T. Barnum Show.

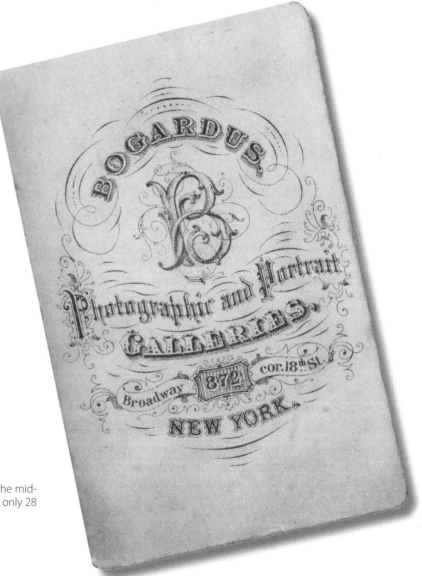

BOGARDUS,
Photographic and Portrait
GALLERIES,
Broadway 872 cor. 18th St.
NEW YORK.

Credit card-sized carte-de-visite (CDVs) were all the rage during the mid-1800s. This one is of little Nellie Keeler, an albino midget billed as only 28 inches tall and shown by P. T. Barnum. Author's CDV collection.

DUDLY FOSTER

CDV of tiny Dudly Foster by photographer Charles Eisenmann, who is well known for his photographic images of human freaks and dime-museum performers.

Two unused admission tickets to the 1893
World's Fair in Chicago. Author's collection.

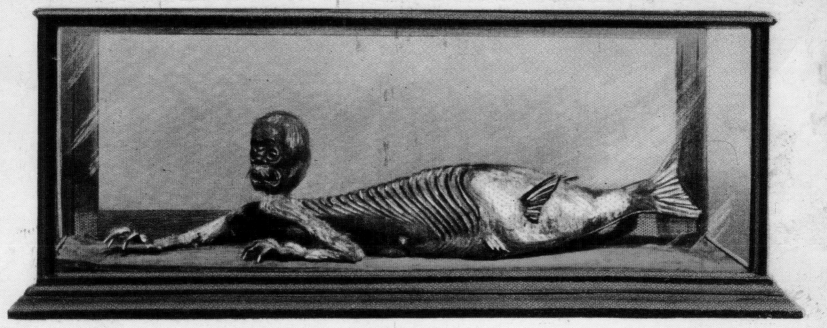

MERMAN ON EXHIBITION AT THE GATOR FARM AND MARINE MUSEUM, HOT SPRINGS, ARK.

MERMAN.

A member of the family of Nereids that inhabited the China Sea many centuries ago. This specimen having been captured in the Gulf of Tonquin, a tributary of the China Sea, off the coast of Quihoy, about five hundred miles from Hong Kong. It belongs to the species of Herbivorous Cetacea, one of the rarest inhabitants of the Sea. Herbivorous Cetacea, occasionally wandered into the more Northern Seas, and invariably caused great excitement among the seamen. In the waters of the Manaar, they were quite frequently seen by Arab and Greek seamen years ago, but they are now almost an extinct type of animal life. This specimen was purchased from the National Museum of China, through the firm of Fook Woh & Co., Importers, San Francisco, Cal, and it is said there are but few others, they being in the large Museums of Europe.

Postcard featuring a Merman, "one of the rarest inhabitants of the sea." Exhibited at The Gator Farm and Marine Museum in Hot Springs, Arkansas. Author's card collection.

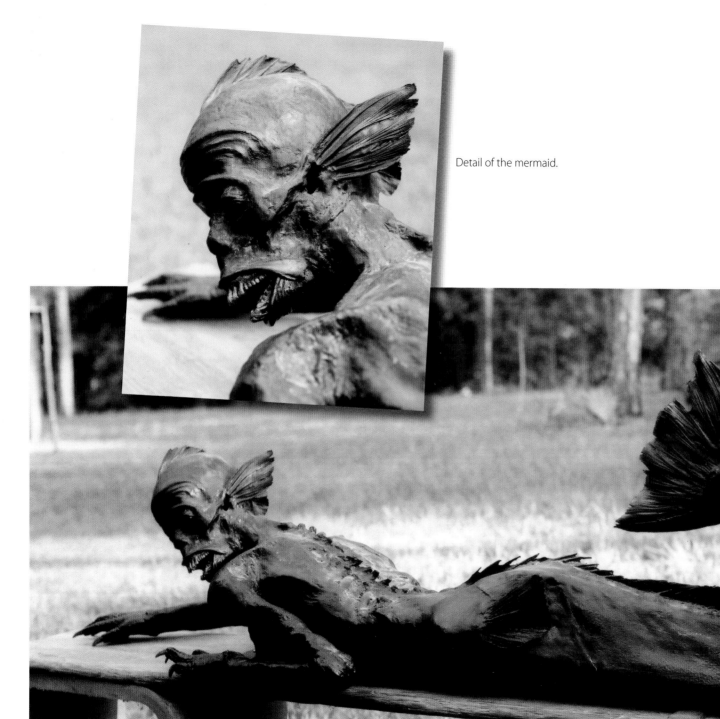

Detail of the mermaid.

Rick's life-sized mermaid.

Medals;—Shells, Corals, and Fossils;

EGYPTIAN MUMMIES,

and ancient Sarcophagi, 3000 Years old; and an entire

Family of Peruvian Mummies;

the DUCK-BILLED PLATYPUS, the connecting link between the BIRD and BEAST, being evidently half each;—the curious half-fish, half-human

FEJEE MERMAID,

which was exhibited in most of the principal cities of America, in the years 1840, '41, and '42, to the wonder and astonishment of thousands of naturalists and other scientific persons, whose previous doubts of the existence of such an astonishing creation were entirely removed;

Elephants and Ourang-Outangs;

ANIMALS and BIRDS of every nation: Sharks, Seals, and a variety of FISHES, including the curious

SAW AND SWORD FISH,

Fejee Mermaid ad from The Barre Patriot, Barre, Massachusetts, 1850.

Cabinet card of an unidentified turn-of-the-century dapper showman and his little prodigy, Princess Wee Wee. Note the ribbons the showman used for his own shoelaces. The cabinet card used a larger photographic image, 4¼ by 6½ inches, than the CDV and became the more popular of the two forms by 1865, although the smaller cards continued to be made until the 1880s. Author's card collection.

Close-up of Princess Wee Wee.

LADY LITTLE. "The Doll Lady"
Height, 28 in.; Weight, 19 lbs.
Born in Basse, Pyrenees, France, Sept. 14, 1897
DREAMLAND CIRCUS SIDE SHOW, C. I.

Pitch card of 19-pound Lady Little, Dreamland Circus Side Shows, Coney Island, New York, 1897.

Early CDV of Myrtle Corbin, the four-legged woman, whose extra legs resulted from a form of conjoined twinning classified as dipygus by the medical profession. Born in 1868, Myrtle had a long career in show business. Author's CDV collection.

CDV of "Waino and Plutano, the Wild Men of Borneo" by photographer Charles Eisenmann. Hiram and Barney toured the nineteenth century show circuit for nearly 50 years as Waino and Plutano. Hiram died in 1905, Barney followed in 1912, and both are buried in the Mount View Cemetery at Mount Vernon, Ohio. Gerry Drewicz CDV collection.

Gerry Drewicz explained to Rick how and why he started collecting images of early sideshow performers. "I happened to notice a couple of Eisenmann photos in a case of an antique dealer. I looked at them and thought, 'Hey, these are the same kind of photos that were in a book I read.' I didn't buy them, but when I got home I couldn't stop thinking about the photos. I realized that these were the actual photos that the attractions personally handled and sold to the people that came to see them. By morning I just had to have them. I got up and went right to the antique dealer. I was delighted to see they hadn't been sold."

Eisenmann, Photo-   229. Bowery, N.Y.

Skull of P. T. Barnum's three-horned steer. Barnum showed this amazing bovine with three eyes and three horns while it was alive. Author's sideshow collection.

Barnum's three-horned steer featured on the circus' 1892 Barnum & Bailey Greatest Show on Earth poster.

Lucia Zaarte, 5 pounds, 20 inches tall, "Greatest Wonder of the Age!" died of hypothermia in 1890 when the train on which she was traveling became stranded in a snowstorm in the Sierra Nevada mountains. Author's CDV collection.

GREATEST WONDER
OF THE AGE!
SENORITA
LUCIA ZARATE!
The Mexican
LILIPUTIAN!
THIS YOUNG LADY IS
12 Years of Age!
20 Inches High!
AND WEIGHS
Only 5 Pounds!
IS PERFECT IN FORM AND FEATURE
☞ TOM THUMB IS A GIANT ! 🙈
COMPARED WITH HER.

This Wonderful Mexican Pigmy; it would be difficult to exaggerate the wonder of this human curiosity. The plain truth makes it strange enough. You must see, hear and feel, and even then you will leave wondering.

Photo by J. WOOD,   NEW YORK.

Carte-de-visite of the exotic Zalumma Agra, Barnum's first "Circassian Beauty." The showman enthralled audiences with tales of white slavery and harem life. The CDV c.1860s was sold as a souvenir at his American Museum in New York City. Author's CDV collection.

2-HEADED CAT

ZALUMMA AGRA,
The Star of the East.

"Titty and Bitty the 2-Headed Kitty," born in 1957, Skidmore, Missouri, and lived for six weeks. They are currently on tour with the Big Circus Sideshow.

Real unicorn skull. Oberon Zell-Ravenheart ("OZ") created nine living unicorns in the 1980s, using techniques pioneered by Dr. Franklin Dove's experiments on horn buds in the 1930s. Dr. Dove transplanted the horn buds of a three-day-old calf from their usual location to the center of the forehead, resulting in a unicorn steer. In 2007, while interviewing OZ, Rick asked if he had saved any of the unicorn skulls. OZ said he knew of two skulls and agreed to photograph them. Skull in Diana Daring collection.

P. T. Barnum cabinet card.

Two-headed puppies, born in 1946, Slidell, Louisiana. These unique border collies have four eyes and four ears and reportedly ate with both mouths. They lived for seven weeks. Originally displayed in a veterinarian's office. Author's sideshow collection.

CHAPTER XV
Carnies, Kin, Cousins & Other Characters
Family and Friends On and Off the Midway

My mom, Dottie West (no relation to the country-western singer), ran one of three giant horse shows that I operated across the country. I never publicized how many Big Jims were out there, and nobody took notice until "Big Jim" Thompson ran for governor of Illinois in 1976.

At the time, a couple of my Big Jims were playing fairs in the Prairie State. And at each fair where "Big Jim" Thompson campaigned, one of my Big Jims was there also. The press played up the coincidence, which gave his name recognition a boost. (Maybe that's why he won a record 65 percent of the vote, eh?)

Anyway, I wanted to tell you what happened on a trip Mom took with me in January of 1979. Mom, my cousin Allen, my brother-in-law Joe, three helpers and I left snowbound, minus-ten-below Wisconsin with five trucks and trailers for a winter tour of Texas, Arizona, and New Mexico. Everyone looked forward to warm, sunny weather, and as we drove along we were encouraged to find less snow. However, we soon found plenty of ice.

Before we reached Urbana, in eastern Illinois, the dangerous ice-covered roads had affected travel so much that most of the gas stations and convenience stores closed. Nevertheless, my animals needed water, food, and rest, and the trucks needed fuel. (Every six hours, we break to care for the animals and gas up.) We kept moving to locate a truck stop that was open.

Rick's mom, Dottie West, and Big Jim the Giant Horse at the Pima County Fair in Tucson, Arizona, 1978.

Food, water, Bible readings keep Fair-sized Belgian horse content

Belgian gelding Big Jim towers over West

"Another 50 miles, and we'll be out of this," I thought. Normally, I drive 60 miles per hour, but on the glare ice our caravan crawled along at 35 mph. Because most of the gas stations were closed, I drove ahead to locate one still open for business.

After finding one, I alerted the rest of the crew to my location on the CB radio. We fed and watered the animals, fueled up and, two hours later, got back on the road. As the storm continued to force drivers off the highway, we proceeded into the night. Before midnight, we pulled into a brightly lit truck stop, unloaded and bedded down the animals, and slept about six hours.

In the morning, after loading the animals into the trailers and warming up the truck engines, we encountered another obstacle. The warmth of all eight tires on each truck/trailer rig had, during the night, melted half-moon cups into the inch-thick ice covering the parking lot. As drivers pressed on the accelerators, the truck tires just spun in the ice cups. Nothing moved. We couldn't even budge the trucks by shifting from drive to reverse, trying to rock them back and forth. Each truck was stuck.

Fortunately, I had brought along a four-wheel-drive truck. Using a tow chain, I pulled one truck out of its ice cups. Then I pulled another loose until I had the entire five-vehicle caravan rolling. Once on the road we seemed to be the only vehicles moving along Interstate 57. We even passed an ice-covered, abandoned county snowplow that had been salting the road before the driver apparently lost control and spun into a ditch.

The crew gathers for a photo opportunity before heading south.

The massive ice storm persisted for a day and a half all the way to Dallas. Each time we stopped, our trucks became stuck again. These were the worst driving conditions in which I ever pulled trailers, and to this day I can't believe we got through without putting something in a ditch.

Joe, Conley, and Rick working a shopping center date in south Texas.

Ice-covered shopping center parking lot in Dallas. And Rick thought it was going to be warm in Texas!

After we arrived in Dallas, Joe and I set out to book some additional spots to add to the livestock shows already booked. We picked out towns with populations of 15,000 or more, drove to them, and checked out the shopping centers and malls. We booked the ones we liked the best and set up newspaper advertising, running one ad the week before our shows arrived and two more ads during the week of the show. We also took care of electrical hookups and, within two weeks, booked our target goal of thirty spots, each lasting seven to ten days, in Texas, New Mexico, and Arizona.

At this point, we split up. Some exhibits went to one town while others were booked to another. I took one Big Jim exhibit one place while Mom left with hers.

The Big Jim horse that Mom showed was actually named Ben. He might not have been the biggest horse we ever showed, but my mom was sure of one thing: Ben was the prettiest. Ben's roan coloring—red with gray hairs—was magnificent.

My mom read Bible verses to "Ben Boy," as she called him, every morning. She said the Good Book made him content. "I'm a Christian woman and Big Jim is a Christian horse," the *Arizona Daily Star* (Tucson) quoted Mom as saying while she was playing the Pima County Fair.

When a horse puller gave my mom some lip about how big Jim was, Mom let the man know he was treading on unfamiliar ground when she stated in no uncertain terms, "Big Jim's the prettiest horse you'll ever see!"

"Oh, that's right, ma'am," the puller agreed, sensing it was time to make a hasty exit.

My mom, Dottie, loved that magnificent horse and kept him looking that way. She even used Pledge® furniture polish on his tail and mane to keep them tangle-free. Mom received many offers to buy Ben over the years, but no offer was good enough for her "Ben Boy."

"The Giants are Here!" An example of the different newspaper ad layouts used to advertise still dates.

I love olive-burgers. And no one seems to make them better than Bob and Betty's Food Trailer. That's where I met Alan Hogan—at the Mecosta County Fair in Big Rapids, Michigan, during the late 1980s.

Alan worked at the trailer where olive-burgers and giant onion rings headlined the menu. After they shut down for the night, Alan practiced with his boomerang in the fair's parking lot. Since I exercised the animals in the same parking lot each evening, we saw each other regularly.

I realized that Alan wasn't afraid of any kind of work. With the food trailer's tour winding down, Alan became a natural candidate to run my Miniature Horse Show. However, he didn't have a driver's license; it had been revoked for drinking and driving. So we petitioned the judge, asking him if he would grant Alan an exemption to drive for Star Farm (that's me).

The judge agreed and wrote Alan a letter allowing him limited driving privileges. After one year of showing the miniature horse, Alan ran one of my Big Jim exhibits, and he did great. The horse and barn never looked better. The judge's letter remained folded in his wallet—becoming tattered and torn—for the four years he drove for me.

For six years, Alan has lived and worked in Antarctica as part of a scientific research support team. I do believe he is the only person in the world to intentionally go skinny-dipping in Antarctica, too. To get into the water, he had to break through the ice. I know it's a little hard to believe, but Alan sent me a homemade video to prove it.

Following his last eighteen-month tour, Alan got off the Ice (Antarctica) and headed to China. Shortly after arriving there, he sent the following email:

Greetings, Comrade Rick. How's life in the decadent old United States? I have been in Beijing for ten days. Way frickin' cool!

My life seems very surrealistic. I mean, one day I am on top of a 200-foot tower at the South Pole with temperatures at minus 60-70 degrees. The next thing I know I'm laying on my back on top of a 2,000-year-old watchtower on the Great Wall watching a meteor shower with two, 24-year-old Chinese girls.

My life seems too strange. I was flying my kite at Tiananmen Square the other day, and I became a tourist attraction of sorts. People were coming up to feel my hair and touch my tattoos. Many times I had to stop for people who wanted their picture taken with me. I guess blond, longhaired carnies with tattoos are rather rare here in the Peoples Republic.

Alan pointing to the marker for the South Pole, 2001. Each year a new marker must be positioned as the ice is always moving.

Oh, if you are still doing stonework around the farm, save a little space somewhere. I sent two small stones from the Great Wall to you.

Sure enough, Alan sent a package postmarked from China with two rocks in it. And I made sure those stones secured a special spot in my cabinet of curiosities. Alan also sent stones from Antarctica to accompany the stones I collected during my Kenyan trip to become a part of my stone fireplace.

Jimmy Daniels, former county commissioner, self-proclaimed glitter-babe magnet, bull's-eye pistol-shooter, and the "Prince of Redneck Rock," painted and lettered my first Giant Hog Show.

I first met Jimmy in 1983 when I was having trouble with my Colt .45 auto feeding cartridges. I heard Jimmy knew a thing or two about .45 auto pistols and was hoping he could work some voodoo pistol magic to get it rocking and rolling again. He came through for me, and we did a little shooting together.

Jimmy, a bull's-eye shooter, believes the only way to hold a pistol is with one hand. I guess that's okay if you're on a horse, because you would need the other hand to hold the reins.

Alan Hogan camping in Antarctica, 2000.

114

I dropped by Jimmy's sign shop in Cushing, Texas, recently to talk about music. Jimmy learned some guitar licks from Stevie Ray Vaughan during the short time he lived in Nacogdoches, Texas. After Vaughan moved, Jimmy formed The Jimmy Daniels Black-Label Band, which promised his fans "music to which they could dance or your money back." He now plays lead guitar with a new band, The Short Fuse Blues Band.

I met Jimmy's puppy, Bonnie Parker. While playing with Bonnie, I discovered the tan mutt had six toes on her feet. She would have been a star in a sideshow during the 1960s, no doubt about it!

They would have advertised her on a big banner in front of a 10-in-1 freak animal show, along with a four-winged duck, five-legged cow, two-headed turtle, hairless dog, and other freak animals.

Bonnie Parker, the dog with extra toes, owned and shown by Jimmy Daniels, the Prince of Redneck Rock!

When I was ten years old, I constructed a bicycle built-for-two. I cut apart two used bicycles—a boy's and a girl's—and needed someone to weld them together. That's how I met Clarence Heidgen.

Clarence owned a blacksmith shop at 115 S. Broadway in Green Bay, Wisconsin, and gave me my first welding lesson in 1958. Over the years, I spent many hours at the shop listening to Clarence's tales. His grandfather, Matt, started the blacksmith shop in 1865, the year the Civil War ended, and died there. Clarence's dad, John, died at the shop, too, while working at the same anvil I used. I guess that's why Clarence thought he would work at the shop until his final day, too.

In the old days, carriages were built at the shop and then painted on the second floor where there was less dust. A pulley system was installed to hoist them up. Clarence's dad and grandfather shoed horses there, too. The rings used to tie the horses were still attached to the walls, even though no horses had been shod since Clarence took over the shop in 1936.

Jimmy Daniels in front of Rick's freshly painted Giant Pig show.

Pieces of iron, old wheels, horseshoes, broken chain, a kid's sled, busted tools, and other parts, some from the turn of the century, were piled and hung everywhere. Each piece of junk had its own story, including the tools.

Two large several-hundred-pound metal anvils were mounted on maple tree stumps on the floor, one in the front of the shop and one next to the forge. The anvils were used to work heated metal, along with a shear, metal bending jig, welder, a coal forge, and water tank for cooling the metal. I loved to look through the old parts and ask Clarence about them.

Clarence taught me how to weld and use the forge. He let me use the shop at night and on Sundays, providing me with my own key. Sometimes a customer brought something in to be fixed while I was working on one of my many projects. If I could, I would fix the item and put the money paid in Clarence's "secret" money drawer.

When folks brought in things to be fixed, Clarence would say, "When do you need it... yesterday, I suppose?" Customers thought everything they brought in to be fixed at the blacksmith shop had a lifetime warranty. If their gizmos ever broke down again, they expected them to be fixed for free, even stuff that was already worn out.

When I turned 15, I bought a rusty old 1929 Ford Model A Tudor sedan, which had no roof or windows. First, I completely restored it to like-new condition. Later, working at the blacksmith shop, I installed a V-8 engine, transmission, and a rear end scavenged from a wrecked '56 Chevy BelAir. I kept tinkering with it, finally putting in a 327-cubic-inch Corvette engine with 375 horsepower. I also added a roll bar so I could drag race at the local track. (After I turned 21, I sold the hot rod.)

A newspaper clipping that Clarence mailed Rick showing Clarence in front of the blacksmith shop, 1987.

Clarence working at the blacksmith shop, 1965.

Uncle Pat helped Rick haul home his prize 1929 Ford sedan, 1963.

Rick's Ford Model "A" hot rod, 1968.

Clarence died a few years back. No, he didn't die at the blacksmith shop, like his grandfather and father. In 1993, the shop was torn down to make way for a parking lot. A sacrilege! The shop should have been turned into a museum.

I'll never forget those hours spent with Clarence at the shop where I built some of my shows, installed trailer hitches, and made repairs to my equipment. I still cherish the old cross-peen hammer that Clarence gave me when I turned 16. Clarence even made a set of shoes for Big Jim, my giant horse.

Clarence once told me, "There's only two reasons a blacksmith goes to hell: one, for working cold iron, and the other, for not charging enough." He always nagged me for not using the forge to heat the metal before bending it. His death caught me by surprise. Some things were left unsaid; I really miss that old blacksmith.

Nate Kern was young, tall, and handsome, and worked for me several years after graduating from high school. He was not a womanizer and didn't use his attributes to lead women on.

When we played the Lake County Fair in Crown Point, Indiana, a pretty, dark-complexioned, dark-haired gypsy girl with a yen for Nate hung around my Giant Horse Show all week. She worked in a "mitt joint" (fortune-telling booth) nearby and hoped to see Big Jim (and Nate, too, of course) for free.

She offered to tell Nate his fortune in exchange for a look at Big Jim. As cool as could be, Nate told her he also could tell fortunes and wanted to know if she wanted to hear hers.

"I didn't know you could tell fortunes," she said excitedly. "Yes, tell me mine!"

Nate picked up her hand, pretended to read her palm, paused about 10 seconds and looked her in the eyes. "You're not going to see Big Jim for free," he deadpanned.

The gypsy girl's eyes flashed, and she stormed off down the midway, not to return the rest of the fair.

During the early 1980s, I bought a mechanical bull resembling the one used by John Travolta in the movie, *Urban Cowboy*. I named the bucking contraption "Sugar Velvet," and asked Nate to run it for me. The bull made a great deal of noise, and I tied an eighth-inch-thick steel cowbell to the bull to draw even more attention. As the bull spun and bucked, the cowbell's clapper slammed frantically against its steel shell, resonating a loud invitation throughout the fairgrounds.

To complete the allure of the mechanical bull, Nate and I wore cowboy hats, boots, and belts with picturesque buckles, and even learned how to ride Sugar Velvet while standing on its back. When Nate turned it on, I mimicked being on top of a real animal, yelling, "Whoa, boy!" We attracted attention, all right!

To add an element of realism to our show, I found a rodeo buzzer that went off after someone stayed on the bull for eight seconds, but we didn't use the buzzer much. Most of the time, the rides lasted under three seconds.

Whenever a good-looking girl mounted the bull, we operated our creature slowly so she could stay aboard several minutes, suggestively turning her from one side to another. "Ride him!" I yelled, while Nate nudged the controls to cause Sugar Velvet to seductively buck and turn.

After we filled our area with an appreciative crowd, we put the girl's boyfriend aboard. Within a couple of seconds, Nate goosed the mechanism and caused the bull to buck violently, flinging the unsuspecting victim high into the air. He didn't even get a ride! And everyone started teasing him.

"Hey, she rode it for several minutes, and you can't stay on for two seconds!" one wisecracker laughed.

The boyfriend paid to ride again. His male ego couldn't resist the challenge. He had to prove to the assembled crowd that he could ride Sugar Velvet. We took it easier on him—but only for a few seconds—before we unceremoniously dumped him again.

His girlfriend looked down at him in dismay and asked to ride the bull again to show him how it's done. Of course, we obliged, and each time either one rode the contraption, he had to cough up two bucks!

Nate and I had a couple of other little routines that we did. As I would start to get on the bull, Nate spun it toward me, then backward, and paused as if Sugar Velvet was a real bull. I bellowed, "Whoa, Sugar Velvet, easy boy!" and feigned nervousness as I tried to get back on.

Sometimes when I rode, Nate stopped the bull, and I walked to its nose and balanced myself, whereupon Nate turned it back on, which tossed me a good ten feet into the air. That was always a crowd favorite.

A motorcycle gang once came over to our bucking machine en masse, wanting to ride the bull. Nate and I were a little nervous and gave the first biker an easy ride. One of the other bikers plunked down another two bucks and growled, "Turn that bull up and slam that boy down on the mat. I'm paying for this ride."

We dumped him on the first buck of the bull.

All the bikers cheered. All their girlfriends cheered. Hey, these folks were fun!

The bikers partied and rode Sugar Velvet all night, the rougher the better. And we had so much fun that we gave their girlfriends some of the sexiest, slow rides anyone could ever have imagined.

I worked with both my cousins, Wayne and Jerry Pies, at one time or another. Wayne is my age and the luckiest person I know. Whenever he shoots pool or plays cards, he wins. If Wayne and I were to bet on the color of the next car coming around the corner, he would win repeatedly.

Let's say you flip a coin. There's nothing you can do to influence the coin toss. The probability of which side comes up doesn't vary, right? It is always 50/50. So I ask myself, "Why does Wayne win all the time?" I don't know how it works, but Wayne wins.

Rick practicing tricks on his bucking machine.

119

Cousin Wayne Pies and girlfriend Joanne working Wayne's Miniature Horse Show at the Saint Joseph County 4-H Fair in South Bend, Indiana, 2001.

Let me give you an example. Wayne bought five acres in Bradenton, Florida, for $25,000. In order for the power company to run a line across the back of his property, five live oak trees had to be cut. Wayne negotiated a payout of $5,000 per tree, a total of $25,000, which meant he got back all his money. Therefore, he managed to get five acres for free. But that's not the end of the story. Wayne sold the property before the trees were cut, netting him even more money. Now, that's lucky!

Wayne and I grew up together, and the first giant horse I showed belonged to him. We used Wayne's horse and bookings and my truck, trailer, and portable barn. Wayne helped me out on a few other occasions, and his dealings have always been more than fair. In fact, he is one of the most generous people with whom I have ever done business.

During the early 1970s, Wayne heard that Tom Johnson's Redwood Log House was for sale. The exhibit consisted of a giant California redwood log, eight feet in diameter and thirty-five feet long, hollowed out by hand and converted—with the bark still attached— into an exquisite four-room

house, complete with bedroom, bar, and kitchen. The log house was then mounted onto a specially built semi-trailer.

Johnson's price for the display, including the tractor, was $40,000. He told Wayne he would take $5,000 down and let him pay out the balance in installments. Since Wayne didn't have the entire cash down payment, Johnson wanted to know if they, at least, had an agreement. Wayne said yes, and they closed the deal with a handshake.

Johnson told Wayne he was scheduled to play the Canfield Fair in Ohio the following week and said he could pick up the display by handing over the $5,000 down payment in Canfield. He also agreed to run the display for Wayne at the fair and apply the proceeds toward the down payment.

Wayne was somewhat nervous about the purchase since $40,000 was a lot of money in 1973, so he enlisted my Uncle Tom as a partner. Here's where the story gets strange: When Wayne went to pick up the log house at Canfield, Johnson told him the log had taken in nearly $5,000, amounting to the full down payment. I told you Wayne is lucky!

A couple months later, Wayne rounded up the remaining $35,000 in cash, placed it inside an old suitcase and hitchhiked from the Washington Parish Fair in Franklinton, Louisiana, to the Mississippi State Fair in Jackson to pay off the balance, proving Wayne's handshake is as good as any lawyer-written contract.

Wayne and Uncle Tom ran the Redwood Log Display for five years, after which they sold it to Benson's Wild Animal Farm in New Hampshire. When the Animal Farm went bankrupt, a carnival bought the display at auction and completely restored the attraction to its former appearance. The Redwood Log House was then sold to Ripley's Believe It or Not museum for a reported $240,000, and is now on display in St. Augustine, Florida.

Wayne's younger brother, Jerry, and I traveled the Midwest showing one of Uncle Tom's giant steers. On the way from Florida to Griggsville, where we were slated to play the Western Illinois Fair, we crossed the Tennessee state line and I pulled the semi into the state's weight scale for a routine check. At least, that's what we thought.

A uniformed state inspector sauntered out to us and demanded, "Let's see your paperwork, ladies." ("Ladies?"... I knew we were in trouble!)

"What paperwork?" I said. "We don't have any paperwork."

"Well, you're going to have to pay a fine if you don't have a permit," he stated.

"Can't we just buy a permit?" I asked.

"Well, it's a little too late for that, Sonny. You needed the permit before you entered the state," he laughed. "Now pull it around back and c'mon in. You boys gotta pay a fine."

I had no idea someone could take most of our cash legally. Jerry and I had precious few dollars remaining; we barely had enough gas money to reach Griggsville. Three days before the fair, we reached our destination with an empty gas tank, some pocket change, and the souvenir Canadian dollar I saved from my first trip to Canada in 1963.

We had enough feed for the steer, but we needed to figure out how to fill our stomachs until the fair started. ATM machines didn't exist in those days, so we decided to survive on Coke™ and crackers. We thought we could eat the crackers and then drink the soda, causing the crackers to swell up and make our bellies feel full. Scouring the highways, we picked up refundable pop bottles along the road to finance our newly planned diet. We survived for two days this way until some friends who show "Big Willie the Gator" showed up and loaned us some money.

On a separate occasion, Jerry and I were up all night driving the semi to the Henry County Fair in Napoleon, Ohio. After we arrived tired and a little crabby, we got into an argument, about God knows what, while setting up the barn. I turned away from Jerry for a moment, whereupon he picked up a handful of loose, wet cow manure, and flung it at me.

Whap! He plastered me pretty good. Whatever manure didn't splatter across me, wound up on the front of the giant steer barn. I didn't retaliate right then because we had to clean the manure off the show and finish setting up. But I bided my time.

When Jerry disappeared to take a shower, I got my chance. I unzipped his sleeping bag. Then I grabbed the pitchfork, and ran to the steer's stall where I gently scooped up a fresh cow pie, and placed it inside his sleeping bag before zipping it back up. Jerry didn't find it until he slipped into bed later that night!

Do you know what a "cattle hotshot" is? It's a cattle prod that measures a couple feet long with two metal prongs on the working end, powered by six batteries. The device buzzes and can give you a substantial shock.

Anyway, there were times when Jerry had a little trouble getting up in the morning. I learned that if I insert the prod into his sleeping bag just right, Jerry was able to fly about three feet out of that sleeping bag and land on the floor! I gave Jerry a couple of morning hotshots, but I found out that I didn't need to continue. All I had to do was make that thing buzz, and he would fly out of bed fast!

I met Wilbur Adank in 1967. Can it really be that long ago? I was playing the Lake County Fair in Indiana near Wilbur's home in Hebron when he dropped by the Giant Steer Show to introduce himself.

Rick and his cousin Jerry showing "Bozo the World's Largest Steer" at the Heart of Illinois Fair in Peoria, 1965.

Wilbur was about 30 years older than me and said he had a "high-schooled" longhorn steer he wanted me to see. He explained he trained animals and had taught the steer to sit up, walk on its knees, stand on a pedestal while holding a flag in its mouth, say its prayers, and get up like a horse, front-end first. He left, promising to come by and pick me up on Friday at 6 A.M.

A lot of people have told many strange, fictitious tales to me over the years, so I thought this might be one of them. When I heard a knock on my camper door at the appointed time, I was more than surprised; I was still in bed.

"Hey, Rick, you ready to go?" a familiar voice called out. "It's Wilbur."

I rushed to get dressed. Grabbing my camera, we headed over to his Rocking "A" Ranch. Wilbur led the trick longhorn out of his pen, put him through his paces, and I took pictures. They put on a great show, and Wilbur made a lasting impression. He still has one of the black-and-white photos I took that day on his fireplace mantle.

Wilbur putting his educated steer through a routine, 1967.

Wilbur riding his longhorn steer down a country lane.

1967 photo, taken the first time Rick went to Wilbur's Rocking "A" Ranch, as he watched Wilbur work his high-schooled steer.

Wilbur was the originator of the nylon horse halter, but because DuPont owned the patent for nylon, he couldn't patent the halter. When I couldn't find a halter at the tack (horse gear) shop that fit my giant horse Big Jim, Wilbur made one for me.

I have enjoyed many hours listening to Wilbur's tales and horse advice. It's hard to believe how many animals Wilbur has "high-schooled" over the lifetime I have known him.

CHAPTER XVI
Wizard, the Miniature Marvel!
Less Is More

In 1988 a barber friend in Nacogdoches, Tom Smith, and I gassed up my Chevy truck's three 20-gallon tanks, and headed for Georgia to pick up a new addition to my animal menagerie. Sixty gallons of gas translated into a 900-mile stop-for-food-only road trip to visit a special horse ranch in Georgia.

The reason for our journey awaited in an old football-field-size chicken house with stalls down both sides. Mr. Bond, a highly regarded longtime breeder of miniature horses, escorted us down the middle aisle, relating how twenty years ago these little horses couldn't be given away. Now everybody loves these tiny beauties.

The horses we saw were not dwarfs. They were perfectly formed miniature horses, too small for even a child to ride. (At the height of the miniature horse craze one of Mr. Bond's horses sold at auction for $65,000.)

Rick's Miniature Horse Show, 1989.

Mr. Bond introduced Tom and me to Wizard, a cream-colored imp with a dark-brown mane, tail, and lower legs. Six inches of his tail dragged on the ground like a bridal veil. And Wizard's breeding was impeccable: His brother was a trick horse in a nationally known circus.

I sure was finding out a lot about Wizard's bloodline, when Tom accidentally discovered something else. Tom leaned back against Wizard's paddock, and the little stallion took a nip out of Tom's butt. A pinch, really, but Tom felt it, all right!

Hey, this little guy was cute, and I wanted him. After paying for Wizard, I picked up the horse and put him in the bed of my pickup. Through the rear-view mirror, I could see Wizard every time he stretched to see over the truck's sides.

Most cars passing us slowed down as folks inside rolled down the windows and leaned out to get a better look. Some people even honked their horns and waved. When we stopped to eat, everyone noticed how tiny the horse was and crowded around us to examine the miniature marvel.

These days, when we take him out for his daily exercise, Wizard puts on quite a show, jumping and bucking like a miniature bareback rodeo bronco. And to this day, after 16 years, Wizard has never bitten me; however, several of my friends got a little nip when they tried to pet him.

For some unknown reason, Wizard also bites the aluminum red, black, and white "DO NOT TOUCH" sign in his exhibit. Maybe it's because when people ask us if he bites, we can just point to the chewed-up sign.

Wizard is now 18 years old, and he may just outlive me. And talk about popular! Hundreds of thousands of people have paid to view and admire the adorable, little Wizard.

See Wizard, the tiny little miniature horse! He's not a pony or a colt, but a full-grown miniature stallion. A handful of hay and a cup of water is all it takes to feed the little Wizard. A horse smaller than a bale of hay! And he's alive, he's real. A tiny little eighteen-year-old miniature stallion. Every child's dream come true... a horse smaller than a dog. A tiny little horse. A horse with feet smaller than silver dollars. You have to see it to believe it, we didn't believe it ourselves until we saw it. See little Wizard, the miniature marvel!

Tom Smith, a barber in Nacogdoches, Texas, gives Wizard his yearly springtime haircut.

Rick's Smallest Horse Show at the Mecosta County Fair in Big Rapids, Michigan.

Rick and Abby's mini, Thumbelina, rode home in the back of their Jeep Grand Cherokee.

Rick's Australian sheep dog outweighs the new arrival by 10 pounds.

Rick and his brother-in-law, Joe, were partners on "Little Luke the Midget Horse." This was the first trailer-mounted show that Rick framed.

Little Luke was the first miniature horse that Joe or Rick purchased from Mr. Bond, though not the last.

Rick's wife, Abby, and their 19-inch, 40-pound miniature horse.

A wood framed miniature horse pit show.

"Well! What do you think of that?"
Actual photo of regular delivery horse meeting "Teddy the Tiny," the smallest horse in the world, for first time.

Abraham and Straus Toyland, 1909 postcard with miniature delivery wagon pulled by Teddy the Tiny.

Well-known showman and show builder Lee Kolozsy built this "Smallest Horse" exhibit. Lee and Rick's cousin, Wayne Pies, teamed up to get this show on the road. Using Wayne's horse and bookings, they hit the Texas fair circuit, including the Texas State Fair in Dallas. Lee later sold the show to Wayne for $18,000, when he needed to raise capital to frame a circus. The exhibit is still on the road, owned by Rick's uncle, Tom Beimborn.

Bobby Jones' World's Smallest Horse show-front trailer, featuring "Tiny Tim. Alive! Only 10 cents!"

CHAPTER XVII
Bottled Babies
Born to Live!

Although Grandma didn't allow me to see that two-headed baby when I was five years old, I managed to see one later in life. One summer at the Tennessee State Fair, a colorful sideshow banner, "Born to Live," promised to show me a two-headed baby. A baby carriage was parked alongside the entrance door, just in case the infant needed to go outside for a little sunshine and fresh air. ("Born to Live" never means alive, I can assure you. If it's alive, a sign or banner will say "ALIVE" in no uncertain terms.)

The show displayed a "pickled punk" (carny lingo for a bottled baby), a preserved freak human fetus displayed in a two-gallon glass jar of formaldehyde. I took my camera inside and shot some great color slides of the two-headed punk.

Two-headed pickled punk, photographed at the Tennessee State Fair.

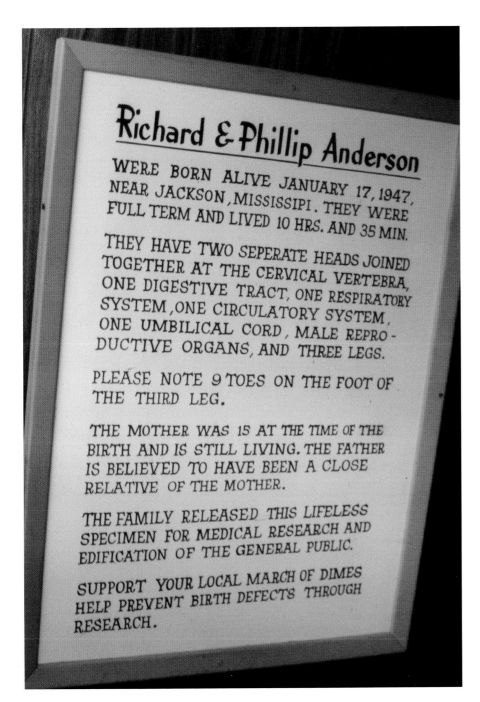

Richard & Phillip Anderson

WERE BORN ALIVE JANUARY 17, 1947,
NEAR JACKSON, MISSISSIPI. THEY WERE
FULL TERM AND LIVED 10 HRS. AND 35 MIN.

THEY HAVE TWO SEPERATE HEADS JOINED
TOGETHER AT THE CERVICAL VERTEBRA,
ONE DIGESTIVE TRACT, ONE RESPIRATORY
SYSTEM, ONE CIRCULATORY SYSTEM,
ONE UMBILICAL CORD, MALE REPRO-
DUCTIVE ORGANS, AND THREE LEGS.

PLEASE NOTE 9 TOES ON THE FOOT OF
THE THIRD LEG.

THE MOTHER WAS 15 AT THE TIME OF THE
BIRTH AND IS STILL LIVING. THE FATHER
IS BELIEVED TO HAVE BEEN A CLOSE
RELATIVE OF THE MOTHER.

THE FAMILY RELEASED THIS LIFELESS
SPECIMEN FOR MEDICAL RESEARCH AND
EDIFICATION OF THE GENERAL PUBLIC.

SUPPORT YOUR LOCAL MARCH OF DIMES
HELP PREVENT BIRTH DEFECTS THROUGH
RESEARCH.

"Life shows," "the unborn shows," "freak baby shows" and "bouncers" are other names used to describe bottled baby exhibits. The babies, or fetuses, are preserved in formaldehyde, usually in glass medical specimen jars, and the pungent smell of the preservative adds to the exhibit's sensation.

At the turn of the twentieth century, people didn't talk about sex education. To make up for the lack of credible sex information, life shows provided real-life visualizations about the birds and the bees, or what really happened when the stork brought an unexpected present to an unwed mother.

Some life shows displayed various stages of human fetal development from conception through eight months, and a lecturer described the development of the tiny human. Perfect specimens gave way to freak shows demonstrating abnormal development, such as when twins don't properly split. One or more freak anomalies, such as six toes, three legs, a frog boy, or a cyclops, guaranteed a much larger attendance and therefore a greater gross. After a while, the anomaly became the show.

Sign displayed inside the Tennessee Punk Show.

Two-headed baby, Pickled Punk Show, 1968.

During the mid-1970s, laws were passed concerning the display of dead babies and fetuses. States prohibited the transport of cadavers across state lines, forcing out the use of real fetuses in sideshows. To conform to new laws, a baby's body was cast in rubber (a "bouncer") and only the model was displayed. Other displays used carefully manufactured imitation baby bodies (also known as "bouncers") with identical dimensions to actual, documented abnormalities.

I saw a wonderful "Right to Life" display last summer at a small county fair in Wisconsin. The usual fetal development models were placed on the front table (the old life shows displayed actual fetuses), and a big sign across the back read, "Stop America's Holocaust." That's the kind of attention-grabber that would have made a great sideshow banner back in the old days.

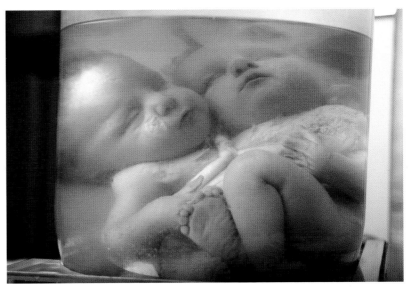

The conjoined twins, 2010. Rick says, "Gee, they haven't aged a bit since I last saw them 40 years ago!"

The tissue damages on the tykes are chemical burns caused by storing the punks in a formaldehyde solution that was mixed too hot.

135

All of a sudden, I stopped cold in my tracks. In front of me was a 20-gallon fish aquarium filled to the brim — not with fish, mind you, but with hundreds of 12-week-old, tiny pink fetuses. It took me a moment to realize they were replicas. You could even get your own little lifelike plastic fetus for a fifty-cent donation!

"Right to Life" display in the commercial exhibits tent. The fish aquarium is filled with life-size, 12-week-old fetuses. Get your own little pink fetal souvenir for a donation of fifty cents!

"It's to educate the children," the attendant told me. Hey, wasn't this the commercial exhibits tent where all the local Main Street businesses put their displays?

I carefully looked over their nonprofit educational exhibit. How very politically correct! If this were a carnival sideshow it would have to be shut down, by God. People would be offended if we allowed this type of thing on the midway. But here, someone took a display that could have come right off the midway, wrapped it up in a neat nonprofit package, and everyone felt just fine. Isn't political correctness wonderful?

Plastic replicas showing fetal development.

Sideshow owner John Strong supplied these photographs of Little Billy, a two-headed bottled baby. Billy was born in 1945 and lived for eight hours. He/they appeared in the movie She/Freak.

Well, pickled punks might be on their way out, but I'm continually drawn to the prospect of a two-headed baby. When I was playing the Tulsa State Fair in 1999, I met John Strong, whose stepfather, Bobby Reynolds, bills himself as "the Greatest Showman in the World" and has owned three different sets of two-headed babies. By the way, 1999 marked my twenty-sixth year at the Tulsa State Fair.

John was exhibiting his own well-worn bannerline... a live freak animal/museum, booked on Jerry Murphy's midway. My four unusual-animal shows were set up on the independent midway. After we met, John explained that the laws used to ban the display of babies didn't apply to his step-dad, as he successfully fought his case all the way through the court system. One court ruled that Bobby's "children" were museum pieces, older than the laws passed to ban their display, thereby legitimizing the exhibition of his two-headed babies.

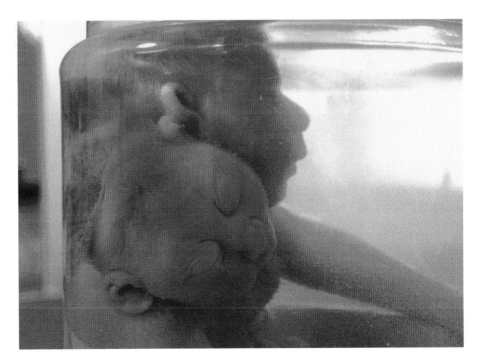

Circus sideshow display featuring bottled two-headed babies.

John and I got to jackpotting about sideshows, and he told me he also owned a real two-headed punk. John also had a young, miniature, black-and-white stallion, which he bought at Lolli Brothers Exotic Animal Auction in Macon, Missouri. I tried to buy the mini from John, but he wasn't selling any attractions.

Nevertheless, it was interesting to visit with John and jackpot about sideshows and his circus career. Come to think of it, that's exactly what you and I have been doing all along, isn't it?

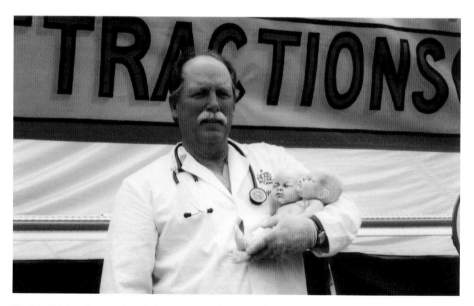

"Dr. West" takes the two-headed wonder out for some fresh air!

Well, let me tell you something. People in the carnival business are always jackpotting, especially when it comes to what their next show is going to be. After all, the next spot just might be a "red" one (carny lingo for the biggest and most profitable spot).

All this talk about sideshows got me thinking about putting together an old-time medicine show. In 1992, I bought an antique Ketterer delivery wagon at the annual carriage auction in Topeka, Indiana. It was built in 1895 by one of the premier commercial carriage builders in New York City, then located on Fifth Avenue and Thompson Street.

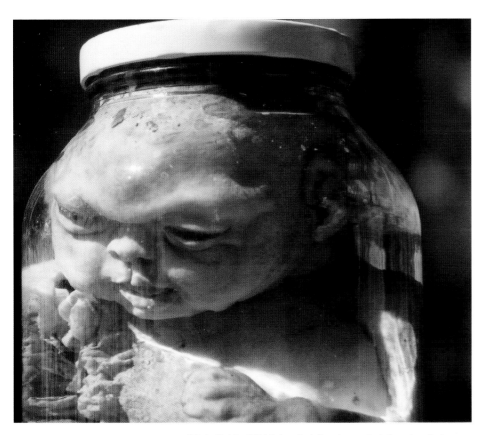

"Little Bobby," Rick's bottled, five-legged, cleft-palate baby.

In April 1992, Rick purchased an antique delivery wagon at the annual spring carriage auction in Topeka, Indiana. The wagon was built in 1895 by one of the premier commercial carriage builders, Kedderer, in New York City. Alan Hogan and Rick spent the winter of 1993 restoring it.

The original Kedderer nametag.

My delivery wagon has the Ketterer metal tag with its name and address attached to the footboard. Alan Hogan and I spent the better part of one winter restoring and painting it hunter green and black. The lettering is done in gold-leaf highlighted in red with black shadow. Hey, I could use this as my medicine show wagon! For my costume, I would put on an old top hat, red vest, black dress pants with a shiny stripe down the side, and some fancy high-top, lace-up shoes.

The restored delivery wagon sporting gold-leaf lettering.

My wife, Abby, would play my lovely assistant. She could dress up like a Persian belly dancer, with see-through harem pants, red vest, finger cymbals, and lots of skin. We would call her Zulanna, Star of the East. My neighbor, Chris, could play the trombone, and I could bang on a brass drum. That would sure attract a crowd.

Watch! Watch! Watch what's going to happen up here! Move in a little closer, folks, it's all free right now, right down front. Get a good spot down front where you won't miss a thing. Don't wait, don't hesitate. The free show's about ready to begin.

As the crowd gathers, I start my spiel:

Ladies and gentlemen, watch while I turn these ten ordinary one-dollar bills you see in my hand into ten twenty-dollar bills, right before your eyes. But first, I'm going to teach each and every one of you a little trick I learned while traveling in the Orient. Now listen carefully. Move your left foot forward, now move your right foot ahead of your left foot, and move your left foot forward again. Did you notice how your body followed? That's right, folks, it's called walking!

Now that we are all gathered down nice and close where you won't miss a thing, I need a victim—I mean, "volunteer"—to assist me. Oh, let me see. Hey, you! Yes, young man with the blue baseball cap, come right on up! Be careful on the steps, son.

The boy is about eight years old and pretty nervous, not knowing what is going to happen next.

What's your name, young man? Bobby, is it? Are you married, Bobby? No? Do you have a girlfriend? You don't? I guess you're still looking for the right young woman!

I notice a little giggling in the audience.

Do you see a girl out in the audience that you might be interested in? How about that one, Bobby? She's pretty cute. I am authorized to perform weddings, you know. We could do it right here on stage.

Bobby, looking at the stage floor, shakes his head no.

Not ready to settle down just yet, I take it?

I address my tip.

I hope you are still keeping an eye on those ten, one-dollar bills. I'll get back to them in just a minute.

I pick up my magic wand, a heavy double-edged, fifty-four-inch sword.

Well, Bob, see this lovely, ornate sword I'm holding up? I am going to attempt to separate your cranium from the rest of your anatomy. What do you think of that, Bob?

Bobby frowns nervously and looks a little confused.

Bobby, this sword is so sharp, you won't feel a thing. Bob, if you would just place your neck on this chopping block. Now, if you place your hands down here—that's right—you will be able to catch your head before it hits the floor.

I blindfold Bobby with a red handkerchief.

I'll be right with you, Bobby. Don't go anywhere; I must find my magic powder. Chris, where's that powder? Bobby, just be patient, please. Zulanna, where is my magic powder? Without my magic powder, I won't be able to reattach Bobby's head... now that's not good for Bobby!

An 1800s pitch card for Ayer's Hair Vigor, a cure-all hair dressing that was pitched from medicine show wagons: "Choice ingredients requisite to produce a preparation which restores gray hair, prevents baldness, preserves and promotes its growth, cures dandruff and all diseases of the hair and scalp, and which forms at the same time, a very superior and desirable dressing. It is entirely free from substances unclean, dangerous to health, or injurious to the hair; and its use is uniformly beneficial, wholesome, effectual and safe."

I pull Bobby to a standing position and untie the handkerchief from his eyes.

As we are unable to locate the magic powder, I will not be able to remove Bobby's head at this time.

Bobby looks relieved.

I guess you're not too disappointed I won't be removing your head today, are you, Bobby? But I want to give Bobby a little something for being a good sport and volunteering to help me.

Taking one of the dollar bills, I hand it to Bobby.

Bob, put this dollar in your pocket. When I change the other nine one-dollar bills into twenty-dollar bills, hopefully your dollar will turn into a twenty, right in your pocket. Not bad for a few minutes work, right, Bobby? Let's give Bobby a big hand. Now watch!

With great concentration, I slowly roll up the nine remaining dollar bills, creating a small tube, and then place the rolled bills in the red handkerchief I had used as a blindfold. I carefully tie it shut using three or four square knots and place it on the chopping block.
Now the real show is ready to start.

Before I continue with the magic [the only magic I do is get the audience's money out of their pockets and into mine], *I would like to tell you a little bit about an unbelievable and amazing wonderment I have available for you today.*

I hold up one of the glass bottles with a cork in the top and a fancy ornate label.

Dr. West's Natural Spring Elixir and Cure-all. It contains the essential ingredients of life and it's all natural.

Of course, it's just bottled water with food coloring added. But heck, water is an essential ingredient of life!

We are all destined to die. From the moment we are born, the clock is ticking away on our appointed time to meet our Maker. Now I ask, which of you would not extend your life if you could? For years, a month, a week, or only a few hours, who would not choose to delay the inevitable?

This elixir contains the essential ingredients needed for life. And for your complete peace of mind, all of our products have a money-back guarantee. Now ladies and gentlemen, I have a special offer for this show. While we normally get $6.00 a bottle, I have been authorized to discount our elixir to the unheard-of, rock-bottom price of $3.00 a bottle, or two for $5.00. Now's the time to make the commitment to start down the road that leads to a long, healthy, happy life.

Opening a bottle of the elixir and taking a big swallow, I exclaim:

Boy, this stuff is great! Now who's going to be first? Thank you, ma'am. Zulanna will make change. Yes, another bottle over here, and two more over there, and another over here, and don't forget to get a bottle or two for your friends and family!

After completing the sale, I hold up the open bottle of the elixir and offer the following toast:

To your health and happiness. And please don't forget our big show this evening, featuring Cowboy Bill with his fast and fancy trick-pistol exhibition. Proudly and perfectly proven to be the greatest act of its kind. He will astound and amaze you with his precision shooting, fast draw, and aerial shooting. Bill will throw six glass balls into the air at one time, then draw and shoot each and every ball before they hit the ground.

He will shoot at the edge of an ordinary playing card and cut it in two with one shot. He will draw a most lifelike portrait of Great Chief Sitting Bull on a copper sheet, using only a .22 rifle. Bill will split a .45 caliber bullet by shooting at the sharp edge of an ax, making the two bullet halves hit two separate bull's-eyes. These are but a few of the many shooting wonders you will witness at the show tonight.

And the lovely Zulanna, Star of the East, will do that dance made famous at the 1893 Columbian World's Fair in Chicago. You have never seen anything like this, and believe me you don't want to miss it! You thought Jell-O had a jiggle... you haven't seen anything yet! But remember, ladies, this is a show for the whole family, entertaining and educational. There is nothing seen, said, or done that would offend the most fastidious young lady in our audience. And it's all free! Bring your friends and neighbors, but whatever you do, don't miss it! You will be talking about our evening show for years to come.

I guess I won't have time to frame the medicine show this season. But it's a great idea, don't you think? Maybe next year. Yeah, there is always next year.

Well, I have come to the end of my little tale. I'm glad you could join me while I rummaged through fifty years of newspaper clippings, memorabilia, and photos of a life spent on the midway. But now I've got to get ready for another summer tour of the fairs. Until then, I'll see you on the midway!

Rick West
Dr. West Traveling Sideshows and Animal Menagerie
Nacogdoches, Texas

CARNIVAL LINGO
And Other Interesting Words and Phrases

AB: *Amusement Business*, the carnival's weekly trade paper.

Aftercatch: An item pitched to the fun-seekers after they already paid to
get into a show. (Photographs, miniature Bibles, a booklet about the
display, a "ring that fits the Giant" were all pitched in sideshows. Toys,
candy, drinks, and magic tricks were also pitched at some shows.)

The Life of General Tom Thumb This miniature
book with gilded edges was published in 1856 and
measures 1 7/8 by 1 3/8 inches. Author's sideshow
collection.

After Show: An added attraction, not advertised on the outside, for which an additional fee is charged.

Agent: The operator of a carnival game.

Backend: The back part of the carnival where the sideshows are located. Sideshows are even referred to as the "backend."

Balloon Store: A dart-throwing midway game in which patrons try to win a stuffed toy by breaking balloons.

Bally or **Ballyhoo**: A free show in front of a sideshow to attract a crowd and entice them into the show. Can also refer to the talker's spiel.

Bally shot of Jim Zajicek's Big Circus Sideshow (BCS) taken at the Florida State Fair. "All I can tell you about the Mystery Man is—when he goes inside and takes off his hood, the young girls will scream, the women will faint, and the men will shout, 'Oh, my God, oh my God!' It's show time!"

Photo taken from behind BCS's bally platform.

Bally Girl: A girl working a free show on the bally platform whose job is to look beautiful, exotic, and draw attention to the bally.

The Curator, the lovely Serpentina (my wife, Abby, plays the bally girl), and Flamo entertain the spellbound tip in front of the Big Circus Sideshow.

Bannerline: A line of banners that form the sideshow's front.

A colorful John Strong banner that was painted by John Hiner, Montgomery County Fair in Conroe, Texas.

Big Circus Sideshow's bannerline.

Banners: Colorful, highly exaggerated canvas paintings depicting the curiosities and wonders to be seen inside sideshows. They are now highly sought after and collected as folk art.

Wonders of World's bannerline.

Barker: Works the bally in front of sideshows and girl reviews. Known in the business as "talker," "spieler," or "grinder."

Beef: A complaint made by a customer about an operation (show, ride, or game). Carnival and fair offices don't like beefs, and will DQ (disqualify, or send packing) any operator for not handling them.

Blank: A spot where you don't make any money.

Blowoff: The end of the show, or an extra-added attraction inside a show for which an additional fee is collected.

"Born to Live": A real specimen that is stuffed, frozen, or bottled, but most assuredly not alive.

Bouncer: A rubber reproduction of a "pickled punk."

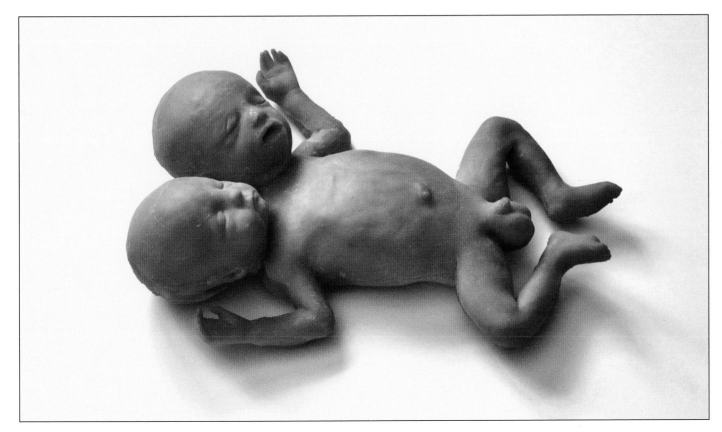

Rubber replica of a two-headed pickled punk, a bouncer.

Call: The time, usually posted at the carnival office, for rides and concessions to open. Also the wisecracks and one-liners used by game agents to entice marks into playing.

Carny or Carnie: Someone who works on the carnival, or the generic name for the carnival.

Chump: Someone who plays the carnival games (see "mark").

Circassian Beauties: The Circassians were reportedly the purest example of the Caucasian race and found living in the mountains surrounding the Black Sea. As the myth goes, these beautiful white women were in great demand for the harems of Turkish sultans. Barnum showed several "Circassian Beauties," starting with Zalumma Agra.

Collecting a Tip: Gathering a crowd.

Concessionaire: A person renting space to do business at the fair.

Cooch or Kooch Show: A basic-as-it-gets girl show with no seating, no comic, and no fancy backdrops. The operator charged an extra fee inside for strippers to peel off everything. The show may also work strong ("to serve lunch"), allowing contact between the girls and the show's patrons for an additional fee. A strong operator could take in as much, or more, money on the inside than the admissions paid at the front ticket box.

Cover-the-Spot: A carnival game in which a "mark" tries to cover a red circle with five zinc metal discs. When the game is run strong, "marks" don't stand a chance.

Norris Welch, the Monkey Man, once told me, "I never gave away a prize the whole time I ran the cover-the-spot game, and I didn't get any beefs either!"

Ding: An unexpected fee, such as when a customer enters a "free" show and is expected to render a donation near the exit, or when a carnival or fair imposes unexpected charges on a concessionaire for camping, electrical tie-in, security, or trash pickup.

One of the Monkey Man's well-used Cover-the-Spot games that he gave Rick while playing the Howard County 4-H Fair.

Do-Gooders: Busybodies who cause games or shows to be shut down in the name of protecting poor town folk, carnival freaks, or show animals from carnies; the "politically correct police."

Dog-and-Pony Show: A small show or operation.

Doniker: Restroom.

Doniker Location: A poor location or space at the fair, where it is impossible to generate any income.

Draw: An advance on one's salary before payday. It wasn't unusual for a carnival employee to need a draw to have money to eat.

Educated or **Learned:** Trained animals, also called "high-schooled" animals.

Flash: Anything done to attract attention, including colorful banners and oversized stuffed prizes.

Flat Store: A carnival game controlled by the operator. (The "marks" can't win this game, unless the operator lets them.)

Floss: Cotton candy.

Framing a Show: To put a new show together.

Freaks: Human or animal physical oddities, such as midgets, giants, or those with three legs or two heads. Humans with physical abnormalities were classified as "Monsters" by the medical profession, but sideshow managers called them "Prodigies."

Front: The front of the sideshow. An exhibitor might say, "I have an eighty-foot front," referring to how much space was needed to set up the show.

Gaff: A fake exhibit or agent-controlled game, e.g. the papier-mâché Arabian Giantess.

Geek: A wild-man show where the performer bites off, or pretends to similarly sever, the head from a chicken, snake, or rat.

Giant Rat Show: An exhibit usually featuring a capybara, or nutria, both South American rodents. The capybara is the world's largest rodent and has been known to tip the scales at 200 pounds.

Gibtown: Gibsonton (near Tampa), Florida, where many carnival people have winter quarters; also known as Showtown.

Rick's wife, Abby, opening their Giant Rat Show.

Going Out Horizontal: Continuing to work until you die, never taking retirement.

Grab Joint: A food stand with no seating (most food stands at the carnival today).

Graft: Crooked games, fixed gambling, pickpockets, and other illegal and dishonest activities.

Grind Show: An attraction that promotes itself continuously. It usually doesn't "bally," e.g. a tape-recorded spiel plays over and over.

Heat Merchant: Someone who creates trouble wherever he or she goes.

High-Schooled: A trained animal; one that was taught to do tricks. Also known as "educated" or "learned."

Hoochie-Coochie: Sexually suggestive dance associated with carnival girl shows, made popular by dancers from the Orient working at the 1893 Columbian World's Fair in Chicago.

Humbug: A hoax, fake, or fraud.

Illusion Show: A sideshow performed by illusion, e.g. "Headless," "Spider-Girl," "Girl in a Fish Bowl," "Snake Girl," and "Girl-to-Gorilla."

Independent Midway: Space that the fair rents out, other than on the carnival.

Jackpot or **Cutting Up Jackies**: Shoot the bull; sit around and tell stories, usually exaggerated, about one's escapades.

Joint: Any concession stand.

Jump: The trip to the next spot (location).

Lecturer: A person who "talks-the-inside" of a sideshow.

Trailer-mounted Headless Woman Show.

Legerdemain: Cleverly executed trick or deception usually requiring manual dexterity, often associated with sleight-of-hand artists and magicians.

Life Show: A bottled baby or fetus show, generally showing monthly development of the human fetus with bottled specimens. Anti-abortion exhibits have similar plastic fetal development displays today.

Location: The assigned space to set up a game, show, ride, or concession.

Lot: The carnival grounds.

Mark: Carnival customers, or "townies," who lose money playing midway games. (An easy "mark" plays until he is broke.)

Postcard of Lou Dufour's Real Two-Headed Baby Show at the 1933 Century of Progress.

Mechanic: A sleight-of-hand artist or card handler; a safety apparatus used during practice to protect beginning flyers or trick horse riders from hitting the ground when they fall off.

Medicine Show: A traveling show usually consisting of one show wagon, typically presenting a small performance until a crowd gathers, whereupon a spiel for patent medicines or cure-alls takes place.

Menagerie: A show where animals are exhibited, rather than performing.

Monkey Day: A term I coined several years ago, referring to nice, fair-weather days with large attendance; a day organ-grinder monkeys could work.

Monsters/Monstrosities: An 1800s medical term used to describe extremely deformed humans, also known as freaks.

Mooch: Sucker or mark.

Sam Staffen used to work at one of my Giant Horse Exhibits before starting a new occupation as agent in a "Balloon Store." At the Coastal Carolina Fair in Ladson, South Carolina, Sam was working the joint strong and made his first big score, taking a mooch for $320. Sam bragged to his boss, who interrupted and asked, "Did the guy have any money left in his wallet when you were finished?" Sam replied, "Sure, I left him with money." His boss responded, "Then you weren't done!"

There aren't many game operators who work that strong any more. Most give out a fair percentage of prizes to keep everyone happy, including the office and the fair board.

Motordrome: A wooden silo where motorcycles, go-carts, or modified cars are driven around a vertical racetrack at high speed. Spectators stand on a platform at the top of the wall and watch riders perform dangerous tricks. In the crowd-pleasing finale, the "money run," the audience shows its appreciation by holding dollar bills (and sometimes $5, $10 or $20 bills) in their fingertips or lips for these daredevils to snatch while racing around the very top edge of the motordrome wall.

Nut: The expenses or rent for a spot.

Back when circuses and carnivals were traveling by wagon, the local sheriff would take nuts off the axles of the show wagons to ensure all bills were paid before the they left town. When the bills were settled, the nuts were returned and the show could leave. At least, that's how I heard the story.

When a showman makes enough to cover his expenses, he has made his nut.

Opening: The initial bally or spiel in front of a show.

Patter: The talk that goes along with a magic trick or an act.

Pickled Punks: Carnival insider lingo for bottled babies.

Picture Gallery: A heavily tattooed man or woman.

Pitch Item: Many performers in sideshows pitch items to the marks for an additional charge. Historically, the freaks pitched photos, "life shows" sold pamphlets, giants pitched their oversized rings, magicians peddled magic tricks, and midgets pitched miniature books and Bibles.

Jim Trover, "The Texas Giant," pitched oversized rings for 26 years while working in circus sideshows. Billed as standing 8'4" and weighing 460 pounds, Jim was born in 1885 in Franklin, Texas. The huge ring is made of white metal and measures 1¼ inches in diameter.

Popper: A trailer selling popcorn, cotton candy (floss), caramel apples, and other sweet treats.

One of Butch Netherfield's flashy poppers.

Possum-Belly-Queens: Derisive term for town girls who fall in love with a carny. Possum bellies are built underneath carnival trucks for storage. In the old days, the ride help slept in these storage areas with their revolving girlfriends. These romances usually lasted only until the last day of the fair.

Privilege: The rent for a concession space at the fair.

Prodigy: A term used by early showmen to describe human freaks, wonders, and oddities; something that is extraordinary or marvelous.

Red One: A very profitable spot.

Revue: Shows that consisted of chorus lines, comics, live music, and a featured exotic. Unlike the standing-room-only "cooch show," a revue would always have seating for customers.

Ride Jocks: The men and boys who set up and run the carnival rides.

Route: The list of spots you are going to play.

Shill or **Stick**: An insider who pretends to be merely a player at one of the carnival games; an insider who pays admission at one of the shows to encourage the "marks" to follow in his footsteps.

Showman: The owner or manager of a show. This term is used today to describe almost everyone in the carnival business.

Single-O: A sideshow with one attraction.

Slough: To tear down or close your operation.

Spiel: The speech made by the talker to entice a crowd into a sideshow.

Spot: A fair; the location of a concession at the fair.

Still Date: A "spot" played other than a fair, e.g. playing strip malls or Walmart® parking lots.

Talker: Known to the general public as a "barker," who gives a spiel on a bally platform in front of the sideshow to gather a crowd (the "tip"), enticing them to buy a ticket (to "turn the tip").

Ward Hall, "King of the Sideshows," working the bally on his "World of Wonders" show. When a paying customer asked if everything in the show was real, Ward replied, "Of course everything's real! Some of it's really real, some it's really fake, but it's all really good."

Tear Down: To take down and load the rides, games, and shows for a jump to the next spot.

Ten-in-One: A sideshow with ten or more attractions on the inside.

Teratology: The medical study and classification of individual malformations, monstrosities, and abnormal wonders (c.1842). The medical profession tried to specifically classify each and every known human deformity.

Thimblerigger: One who cheats by trickery; a swindler or one who runs a fixed game of chance, e.g. the operator of a cups-and-pea con.

Tip: A crowd gathered by the talker in front of a sideshow or attraction. The talker builds, freezes, and turns the tip (gathers, stops, and convinces the fun-seekers to buy tickets).

To Coyote: To steal something.

To Serve Lunch: Allowing physical contact between customers and dancers in a girl show.

To Swing With: To take without the owner's permission; to steal.

Townies/Towner: The local fair patrons.

Turn the Tip: When the talker convinces the crowd in front of a bally stage to buy a ticket and enter an attraction or show.

Universal Ticket System: A system where all tickets are purchased at a central ticket box, not at each ride or attraction. Widespread use hurt attendance and revenues at sideshows.

With It: A person who works on the carnival. (Also expressed as "with it and for it.")

Work Strong: To do whatever it takes to beat the marks, including bribing law enforcement to look the other way.

X: An exclusive concession contract bought from the fair or carnival, e.g. t-shirts, cotton candy, corn dogs.

Yard Note: A hundred dollars.

This is only a small sampling of the many colorful and curious words and phrases used on the carnival midway. New words and phrases are added continuously, some of which become part of the carnies' daily lingo. Many terms are used for one season and then forgotten. Much of the older lingo is no longer in use.

Book List

Anomalies and Curiosities of Medicine, George Gould and Walter Pyle, (New York: Bell Publishing, 1896).

The Book of the Fair—An Historical and Descriptive Presentation Viewed Through the Columbian Exposition at Chicago in 1893, Hubert Howe Bancroft, (Chicago and San Francisco: The Bancroft Co., Publishers, 1894).

Buffalo Bill's Wild West—Celebrity, Memory, and Popular History, Joy S. Kasson, (New York: Hill and Wang, 2000).

A Cabinet of Medical Curiosities, Jan Bondeson, (New York: W.W. Norton & Co. Inc., 1999).

Cabinets of Curiosities, Patrick Mauries, (New York: Thames & Hudson, Inc., 2002).

Carnival Strippers, Susan Meiselas, (New York: Farrar, Straus and Giroux, 1976).

Circus and Carnival Ballyhoo—Sideshow Freaks, Jaggers, and Blade Box Queens, A. W Stencell, (Toronto: ECW Press, 2010)

The Fabulous Showman—The Life and Times of P. T. Barnum, Irving Wallace, (New York: Alfred A. Knopf, 1959).

Fabulous Years—A Showman's Tales of Carnivals, World's Fairs, and Broadway, Lou Dufour, (New York: Vantage Press, 1977).

Freak Like Me—Inside the Jim Rose Circus Sideshow, Jim Rose, (New York: Dell Publishing, 1995).

Freak Show—Presenting Human Oddities for Amusement and Profit, Robert Bogdan, (Chicago: University of Chicago Press, 1988).

Freak Show—Sideshow Banner Art, Carl Hammer and Gideon Bosker, (San Francisco: Chronicle Books, 1996).

Freaks—Myths & Images of the Secret Self, Leslie Fiedler, (New York: Simon & Schuster, 1978).

Giants, Dwarfs and Other Oddities, C.J.S. Thompson, M.B.E., (New York: Citadel Press Book, Carol Publishing Group, 1968).

Girl Show—Into the Canvas World of Bump and Grind, A.W. Stencell, (Toronto: ECW Press, 1999).

James Taylor's Shocked and Amazed! On and Off the Midway, volumes 1-7, (Baltimore: Dolphin-Moon/Atomic Books, 1995-2003).

The Life of P. T. Barnum—Written by Himself, (Originally published in New York by Redfield, 1855, reprinted by University of Illinois Press, 2000).

Monsters—Human Freaks in America's Gilded Age, The Photographs of Chas. Eisenmann, collected and edited by Michael Mitchell, (Toronto: ECW Press 2002).

Mutants—Genetic Variety and the Human Body, Armand Marie Leroi, (New York: Viking Press, 2003)

Mütter Museum of the College of Physicians of Philadelphia, Gretchen Worden, (New York: Blast Books, 2002).

My Very Unusual Friends, Ward Hall, (Ward Hall, 1991).

A Pictorial History of the American Carnival, Joe McKennon, Volumes 1-3, (Carnival Publishers of Sarasota, 1971).

P. T. Barnum—America's Greatest Showman, Philip Kunhardt, Jr., (Alfred A. Knopf, 1995).

Seeing Is Believing—America's Sideshows, A.W. Stencell, (Toronto: ECW Press, 2002).

Shocked and Amazed—On and Off the Midway, James Taylor and Kathleen Kotcher, (Guilford, CT: The Lyons Press, 2002).

Shrunken Heads—Tsantsa Trophies and Human Exotica, James L. Castner, (Gainesville, FL: Feline Press, 2002).

Very Special People—The Struggles, Loves, and Triumphs of Human Oddities, Frederick Drimmer, (New York: Amjon Publishers, Inc., 1973).

Weird and Wonderful—The Dime Museum in America, Andrea Stulman Dennett, (New York: University Press, 1997).

PHOTOGRAPHY CREDITS

About the Author

Rick West was born in Springfield, Missouri, January 18, 1948, to normal parents, as the talkers always said about the human freaks in the sideshows.

When Rick was 5 years old, he attended his first fair, the Ozark Empire Fair, in his hometown.

His family moved to Ashwabenon, Wisconsin, a suburb of Green Bay, in 1953. He attended high school in Green Bay and in Bradenton, Florida, and graduated from the University of Wisconsin Green Bay in 1972 with a B.A. in creative communication.

His sideshow career began in 1960, when his uncle, Tom Beimborn, bought a giant 3,100-pound Holstein steer he named Bozo. Rick got his first taste of carny life that summer showing Bozo at various Wisconsin fairs, including the Wisconsin State Fair.

One of Rick's first shows was a live two-headed calf that he purchased in 1971 from a farmer in Saskatchewan, Canada. Rick builds all his own shows. Over the years he has shown giant steers, gargantuan horses, smallest horses, giant rats, two-headed turtles, Bigfoot creature, giant hogs, mechanical bucking machines, giant lizards, giant alligator, and of course the two-headed cow. In 1994 he framed a food trailer, Rick's Coyote Café, which he also took to the fairs.

After moving to Texas in 1980, Rick took up competitive pistol shooting as a hobby. He competed in many local and several national tournaments, including the IPSC Nationals and the Master's International Shooting Championship, against some of the top shooters in the world.

Finding time from his shows and farm work, Rick and his wife, Abby, founded Abbycadabra Carriage Company in 1993, a horse and carriage service that serves the east Texas area.